Software Lifecycle Support

IT Infrastructure Library

Brian Johnson
Richard Warden

Gildengate House,
Upper Green Lane,
NORWICH, NR3 1DW

LONDON: HMSO

© Crown Copyright 1993

Applications for reproduction
should be made to HMSO

First published   1993

ISBN   0 11 330559 1

ISSN   0956-2591

This is one of the books in the IT Infrastructure Library series. At regular intervals, further books will be published and the Library will be completed in 1993. Since many customers would like to receive the IT Infrastructure Library books automatically on publication, a standing order service has been set up. For further details on standing orders please contact:

HMSO Publicity (PU23 E3), FREEPOST,
Norwich, NR3 1BR
(*No stamp needed for UK customers*).

Until the whole Library is published, and subject to availability, draft copies of unpublished books may be obtained from CCTA if you are a standing order customer. To obtain drafts please contact:

IT Infrastructure Management Services
CCTA
Gildengate House, Upper Green Lane,
NORWICH, NR3 1DW.

For further information on other CCTA products, contact:

Press and Publications,
Room 3/9
CCTA
Gildengate House,
Upper Green Lane,
NORWICH, NR3 1DW.

This document has been produced using procedures conforming to
BS 5750 Part 1: 1987; ISO 9001: 1987.

Table of contents

1.	**Management summary**	**1**
2.	**Introduction**	**5**
2.1	Purpose of this module	6
2.2	Target readership	7
2.3	Scope	8
2.4	Related guidance	9
2.5	Standards	10
3.	**Planning for software lifecycle support**	**11**
3.0	Concepts	11
3.0.1	Interfaces with major management and planning activities	11
3.0.2	Using software lifecycle models	15
3.0.3	Relationship with other IT functions	16
3.0.4	Organizational issues	19
3.1	Procedures	19
3.1.1	Appoint an IT Services Co-ordinator	20
3.1.2	Assessment and selection of lifecycle models	21
3.1.3	Using a software lifecycle model to plan for IT infrastructure management	24
3.1.4	Using a lifecycle model to plan for software maintenance	26
3.1.5	Application to existing systems	29
3.1.6	Documenting IT infrastructure management activity	31
3.2	Dependencies	37
3.3	People	39
3.3.1	IT Services Co-ordinator	39
3.3.2	Staffing requirements	39
3.3.3	Organizing staff	40
3.4	Timing	41
4.	**Implementation**	**43**
4.1	Procedures	43
4.1.1	Running a pilot project	43
4.1.2	On-going procedures	44
4.2	Dependencies	44
4.3	People	45
4.4	Timing	45

5.	**Post-implementation review and audit**	**47**
5.1	Procedures	47
5.1.1	Review of the pilot project	49
5.1.2	On-going reviews	50
5.2	Dependencies	51
5.3	People	51
5.4	Timing	52
6.	**Benefits, costs and possible problems**	**53**
6.1	Benefits	53
6.1.1	Benefits of a pilot project	53
6.1.2	Long-term benefits	53
6.2	Costs	55
6.3	Possible problems	56
7.	**Tools**	**57**
8.	**Bibliography**	**59**
8.1	References	59
8.2	Further reading	59

Annexes

A.	**Glossary of terms**	**A1**
B.	**A 'What could go wrong" scenario**	**B1**
C.	**Lifecycle model descriptions**	**C1**
C.1	Introduction	C1
C.2	The waterfall model	C2
C.3	The spiral model	C4
C.4	Evolutionary and rapid prototyping models	C7
C.5	Summary	C11

Table of contents

D.	**Assessment and selection of lifecycle models**	**D1**
D.1	Introduction	D1
D.2	Systems attributes	D1
D.3	Assessment of existing models	D4
D.4	Selection of a lifecycle model	D5
D.5	Modification of a lifecycle model	D6
E.	**Procedures for application to existing systems**	**E1**
E.1	Introduction	E1
E.2	Document and assess the current situation	E1
E.3	Enhancing strategies	E2
E.4	Systems improvement work required for a new lifecycle strategy	E3
F.	**Effects on specific infrastructure management functions**	**F1**
F.1	Introduction	F1
F.2	Planning and Control for IT Services	F1
F.3	Quality Management for IT Services (QMFITS)	F2
F.4	Managing Facilities Management	F3
F.5	Service Level Management (SLM)	F4
F.6	Capacity Management	F5
F.7	Contingency Planning	F6
F.8	Availability Management	F7
F.9	Cost Management for IT Services	F8
F.10	Configuration Management and Change Management	F9
F.11	Problem Management	F10
F.12	Help Desk	F11
F.13	Computer Operations Management	F12
F.14	Unattended Operating	F13
F.15	Testing Software for Operational Use	F14
F.16	Software Control and Distribution	F15
F.17	Quality Management	F15
F.18	Security	F16

IT Infrastructure Library
Software Lifecycle Support

G.	**Software metrics**	**G1**
G.1	Importance	G1
G.2	When to measure	G1
G.3	Metrics database	G2

Foreword

Welcome to the IT Infrastructure Library module on **Software Lifecycle Support.**

In their respective areas the IT Infrastructure Library publications complement and provide more detail than the IS Guides.

The ethos behind the development of the IT Infrastructure Library is the recognition that organizations are becoming increasingly dependent on IT in order to satisfy their corporate aims and meet their business needs. This growing dependency leads to growing requirement for quality IT services. In this context quality means 'matched to business needs and user requirements as these evolve'.

This module is one of a series of codes of practice intended to facilitate the quality management of IT services and of the IT Infrastructure. (By IT Infrastructure, we mean organizations' computers and networks - hardware, software and computer related communications, upon which application systems and IT services are built and run). The codes of practice will assist organizations to provide quality IT services in the face of skill shortages, system complexity, rapid change, growing user expectations, current and future user requirements.

Underpinning the IT Infrastructure is the Environmental Infrastructure upon which it is built. Environmental topics are covered in separate sets of guides within the IT Infrastructure Library.

IT infrastructure management is a complex subject which for presentational and practical reasons has been broken down within the IT Infrastructure Library into a series of modules. A complete list of current and planned modules is available from the CCTA IT Infrastructure Management Services at the address given at the back of this module.

The structure of the module is, in essence:

* a **Management summary** aimed at senior managers (Directors of IT and above, typically down to Civil Service Grade 5), senior IT staff and, in some cases, users or office managers (typically Civil Service Grades 5 to 7)

* the main body of the text, aimed at IT middle management (typically grades 7 to HEO)

* technical detail in Annexes.

IT Infrastructure Library
Software Lifecycle Support

The module gives the main **guidance** in sections 3 to 5; explains the **benefits, costs and possible problems** in section 6, which may be of interest to senior staff; and provides information on **tools** (requirements and examples of real-life availability) in section 7.

CCTA is working with the IT industry to foster the development of software tools to underpin the guidance contained within the codes of practice (ie to make adherence to the module more practicable), and ultimately to automate functions.

If you have any comments on this or other modules, do please let us know. A **Comments sheet** is provided with every module. Alternatively you may wish to contact us directly using the reference point given in **Further information**.

Thank you. We hope you find this module useful.

Acknowledgement

The assistance of Richard Warden (under contract to CCTA from the Centre for Software Maintenance Ltd) is gratefully acknowledged.

Section 1
Management summary

1. Management summary

This module of the IT Infrastructure Library is currently unique in that it cannot from the outset be used as a simple reference manual. To fully appreciate the concepts described it is necessary to read the module in its entirety. The management summary can only begin to offer a flavour of what is described in the remainder of the module.

The module prescribes closer co-ordination between customers of IT services, IT infrastructure managers and software developers with the ultimate goal of ensuring the provision of quality IT services which meet the demands of the business. This module reinforces the many benefits (eg building in security and quality) obtained from the adoption of structured methods of software development and extends those benefits by promoting a culture in which the needs of the business are met fully by close co-operation throughout the lifecycle of software development.

Co-ordination

In an IT Directorate, customer demands are met through: the development of new systems; the running and maintenance of live IT services; and keeping them aligned with changing business requirements. When IT infrastructure management staff are involved in system development they can ensure that the requirements are met for running and maintaining the proposed system as part of the delivery of IT services. The activities of customer involvement, software development and maintenance can be co-ordinated as a single approach, software lifecycle support. It provides opportunities to incorporate good practice at an early stage in development, to reduce running costs and manage change throughout the software lifecycle; from its design to decommissioning.

In the concept of a software lifecycle, a long-term view of the development, maintenance and enhancement of software is taken. It is important that software developers and IT infrastructure managers are aware that IT services provided to customers are dependent on both parties understanding the customers' requirement, understanding mutual constraints and working together to deliver the best possible IT services. A co-ordinated approach to the software lifecycle:

* incorporates IT infrastructure management requirements at the design and development stages

* ensures that legacy systems are correctly assessed and decommissioned

The IT Infrastructure Library
Software Lifecycle Support

* helps to deliver systems which meet service level requirements
* facilitates opportunities to consider new technology solutions and hence re-engineer the business
* helps to deliver and maintain systems which enable and encourage changing business objectives over an extended economic life
* reinforces security and quality requirements at an early stage
* co-ordinates IT infrastructure management with development and maintenance so that systems are not only designed for maintainability, but are supported fully throughout their lives.

Benefits

In the long term, it is reduced cost of IT service provision that is the crucial issue. Other major issues to the business customer include the quality of IT support, faster and more reliable provision of new or changed application software and reduced risk that software development or change will fail and cause disruption. Using both structured methods and software lifecycle support processes enables both security and quality to be built in to software products thereby reducing overall maintenance costs and improving the quality of delivered services to customers. Their use also facilitates the building-in of interoperability, portability of systems and openness through standards. The costs of involving IT service customers and IT infrastructure managers in software development will be more than offset by reduced costs in providing and maintaining IT services over their lifetime. Additionally, the business customer benefits from the provision of more reliable and flexible IT services.

A co-ordinated approach to software lifecycle support contributes to the economic provision of IT services by:

* significantly improving the communications between IT groups who, traditionally, have worked in isolation
* reducing overall running costs of development and maintenance work (the maintenance part of the lifecycle is the major lifecycle cost and presents a considerable opportunity for overall cost savings)
* improving the overall quality procedures and productivity of the IT Directorate

Section 1
Management summary

* reducing problems when introducing new systems into live IT services

* contributing to better economic appraisal of systems and improved estimation of the service costs to the customer

* providing IT project managers and service managers with key performance indicators

* providing audit trails through processes which are linked and cohesive

* enabling co-ordinated planning for security throughout the system lifecycle

* enabling the identification of trends in service management which will assist in the planning of future systems (interoperability, portability, open systems).

Summary

The **Software Lifecycle Support** module stresses the need for communication between customers of IT services, software developers and IT infrastructure managers, the need for each to understand the requirements of the other and how those requirements can be identified using software lifecycles. The module describes how adopting the use of software lifecycles will assist in the planning and monitoring of projects which meet business objectives.

This module therefore focuses on culture change, changing the way people work, rather than on introducing new activities as in modules such as **Problem Management** and **Help Desk**. New activities are discussed, but the activities can be, for the most part, carried out using existing staff and by adaptation of the current IT organization.

Management issues

The introduction of software lifecycle support procedures often necessitates new ways of working in an organization. The key issues for IT infrastructure managers are:

* effective infrastructure support requires that IT infrastructure managers communicate with software developers and have knowledge of the lifecycle stages of development and maintenance

* management of the introduction of new software systems to the IT infrastructure needs to be planned and implemented so that service levels can be maintained in a cost-effective manner

The IT Infrastructure Library
Software Lifecycle Support

* for consistency and understanding software developers and software maintainers should use the same management structures, methods and tools, and have the same interactions with the IT infrastructure managers

* maintenance must be planned, designed and implemented at every stage of the development process.

2. Introduction

A simple definition of the word 'lifecycle' could be the time period between starting and finishing an activity of some sort; however a software lifecycle is usually defined in a more complex (or comprehensive) way.

What is a software lifecycle?

A software lifecycle is a representation of the complete lifetime of a software system from initial conception to final decommissioning. A projected lifecycle can be used for planning purposes. It is the sequence of stages through which software systems pass. The lifecycle covers the following stages:

* the starting point - when the software specification is first written

* the software development lifecycle - the period of time that begins with the decision to develop a software product and ends when an acceptable product is delivered for implementation as part of live IT services (this time period includes testing and acceptance of the software)

* software maintenance - the modification of a software product after delivery, to correct faults, improve performance or other attributes (enhancement) or to adapt the product to a changed environment

* decommissioning - the point at which the software is no longer useful to the organization.

What is software lifecycle support?

Software lifecycle support is a co-ordinated approach between developers and IT infrastructure management to the activities of supporting software development from its initial design through to its ultimate decommissioning and disposal.

The approach is co-ordinated by using a software lifecycle model which indicates the complete life of a system and provides the opportunity to identify interfaces to IT infrastructure management.

Many organizations use some kind of software lifecycle model (see Annex C for details of such models), but often they only describe part of the overall lifecycle and do not account for all the interactions that may be required

The IT Infrastructure Library
Software Lifecycle Support

between developers, maintainers and IT infrastructure managers. Assessment and selection of the most suitable software lifecycle model for IT systems development means that:

* developers use software lifecycle models which are appropriate to the systems they are developing

* the needs of software maintenance are considered fully during the development phase

* software maintenance is managed and controlled with the same rigour employed in development

* the IT infrastructure management services required to support a software lifecycle model are properly planned and implemented throughout the life of the software system.

2.1 Purpose of this module

The purpose of this module is to provide IT infrastructure management with an understanding of the concept of software lifecycles, to explain how software lifecycles can be used to build in good practice for IT infrastructure managers, and how the lifecycle support processes can improve the quality of delivered IT services to customers. The key message is that software developers and IT infrastructure managers communicate, and where possible co-ordinate, planning for IT service delivery. It is not the aim of the module to take over the responsibility for selection of software lifecycles for development work nor is the message that of interference. Software developers must retain their current responsibilities for software lifecycle selection and associated process modelling. It is simply recommended that other key personnel (IT service customers and IT infrastructure managers) should participate in a co-ordinated approach to the overall planning processes.

A co-ordinated approach

A co-ordinated approach requires careful planning to meld the efforts of IT infrastructure managers, software developers and customers of IT services. Lifecycle modelling is used to identify and document every stage in the life of an IT system and the associated interactions with IT infrastructure activities. The module provides IT service managers with a description of the infrastructure requirements for planning and implementing a lifecycle model which covers all stages of a system's life from project initiation to final decommissioning.

Section 2
Introduction

What information is provided?

Information is given on:

* software lifecycle modelling and task decomposition
* planning the infrastructure support for new software projects and existing systems
* incorporating maintenance requirements into the software development process
* phasing the implementation of new procedures necessary to ensure co-operation between IT infrastructure managers, software developers and customers of IT services.

Clearly, future development projects will provide the most cost-effective opportunities to introduce software lifecycle support: wherever possible, guidance is also given on the application of these techniques to existing systems.

This module is not intended to define one prescriptive solution for software lifecycle support. Every organization will need to develop its own approach to software lifecycle support which can be adopted and adapted to suit individual circumstances.

2.2 Target readership

This module is primarily intended for IT infrastructure planners and IT infrastructure managers, who will need to understand the concepts, the planning issues and the procedures to be co-ordinated.

The module should also be of value to:

* IT development project managers - they will need to know how to plan an integrated approach to a project or a programme of related projects
* software developers and maintainers - they will need to know about the procedures and how they interface to related activities.

IT project managers and software developers will of course need much more detailed guidance (eg about process modelling, process improvement) which is not provided in this module.

The module will also be of interest to those customers who buy or use IT services, who will gain an understanding of the benefits of the approach in improving the quality of the IT services they receive.

The IT Infrastructure Library
Software Lifecycle Support

How to use this module   A full appreciation of the concepts described in this module can be obtained only by reading the entire module. However, an understanding of the context of the approach to software lifecycle support, the underpinning concepts and the major issues can be obtained by reading chapters 1 and 2, and sections 3.0.1 to 3.0.4. Chapter 6 (Benefits, costs and possible problems) is also likely to be of general interest.

The remainder of the module is primarily of interest to IT infrastructure managers and software developers (ie those people who will apply the procedures described in the module).

2.3 Scope

Software lifecycle support provides a bridge between IT infrastructure management and the development and maintenance activities. In particular, it covers:

* project planning (for an individual project or a programme of projects)
* planning for software development and maintenance
* planning for IT infrastructure management and operations.

The module addresses the needs of in-house software development and does not include guidance about:

* use of packaged software
* software developed externally by a third party.

Where an organization retains control of the IT infrastructure and delivery of IT services whilst relinquishing software development to an external supplier, some of the information in this module will be pertinent to planning for the impact of software delivery on the IT infrastructure. In such instances an organization should be assured that software development is undertaken using accepted, preferably structured, methods. This is because the cost of maintaining software is considerable and the cost can be reduced by designing software with maintainability in mind, such that the software runs on the existing IT infrastructure and is easily adaptable to any foreseeable changes to the IT infrastructure.

The organization may desire to specify that third party software development should conform to independent standards such as the DTI Tick-IT initiative. Tick-IT is a

Section 2
Introduction

method by which a software house can be independently audited against accepted international standards and can demonstrate that it has passed and maintained specific quality assurance thresholds in its software production.

The **Software Lifecycle Support** module does not address in any detail how to implement the procedures outlined. This is because IT Directorates differ in their composition and the possible interfaces between infrastructure management, software developers and maintainers are numerous. The module centres on the explanation of the concepts of software lifecycle support and the procedures which can be presented as generalized guidance.

Although the scope of the module is, to a degree, constrained by the needs of infrastructure management, it is extended to include the overall needs of the customer and the long-term impact of IS on that organization.

In terms of the IT infrastructure, close co-operation with software developers and maintainers will have an impact on many of the infrastructure management functions. The module discusses how specific IT infrastructure management services may be affected in a number of ways, which includes the selection of software technologies and tools, and the use of project and quality management systems.

2.4 Related guidance

This module is one of a series of documents issued as the CCTA IT Infrastructure Library. It is part of the Software Support Set. Although this module can be read in isolation, it should be used in conjunction with other IT Infrastructure Library modules.

This module describes interfaces between the modules of the IT Infrastructure Library and software development processes. The major interfaces are dealt with in Annex F. Section 3 and Annex F provide information about specific links between the module and others within the IT Infrastructure Library.

The module covers IT infrastructure management interfaces with other IS/IT management activities which in themselves are covered by other CCTA products such as SSADM, PRINCE and CRAMM.

* SSADM (Structured Systems Analysis and Design Method) is the preferred government systems analysis and design method for the development of IT based information systems

* PRINCE (PRojects IN a Controlled Environment) is the preferred government project management method

* CRAMM is the CCTA Risk Analysis and Management Method, which is designed to help organizations implement policies to provide protective measures for current and future IT developments.

2.5 Standards

BS5515 - Documentation of Computer-based Systems

ISO9001/EN29000/BS5750 Part 1 - Quality Management and Quality Assurance Standards

The IT Infrastructure Library modules are designed to assist adherents to obtain third party quality certification to ISO9001. Such third parties should be accredited by the NACCB, the National Accreditation Council for Certification Bodies.

Section 3
Planning for software lifecycle support

3. Planning for software lifecycle support

3.0 Concepts

This section explains the concepts underpinning software lifecycle support:

* the software lifecycle

* its interfaces with other management and planning activities (3.0.1)

* software lifecycle models and how they are used to plan lifecycle support activities (3.0.2, 3.1.4)

* relationship with other IT infrastructure management activities (3.0.3, 3.1.3)

* the issues that need to be considered when adopting software lifecycle support (3.0.3, 3.0.4, 3.1.2).

3.0.1 Interfaces with major management and planning activities

CCTA is currently refining its guidance about programme management and IT infrastructure planning with a view to publication in 1993. The following is a guide to current thinking and is included to provide a context in which the software lifecycle support processes can be placed.

Figure 1, overleaf, illustrates the major planning activities of software developers, maintainers and IT infrastructure management. It shows the levels of planning for information systems, starting with the business strategy. This sets out the business managers' view of their demand for IT.

Programme management can be viewed as the integration of a series of disparate work programmes, which when managed as a coherent body of work provide benefits to the organization which would not be available were the programmes to be managed discretely. Infrastructure planning (or IT planning) may be the result of examining the IT requirements of each of the work programmes; it is true, however, that infrastructure planning may, in some instances, be in itself a programme of work.

At the highest levels, business and other strategies are studied so that IS strategies and plans are designed to meet the requirements of the businesses.

The IT Infrastructure Library
Software Lifecycle Support

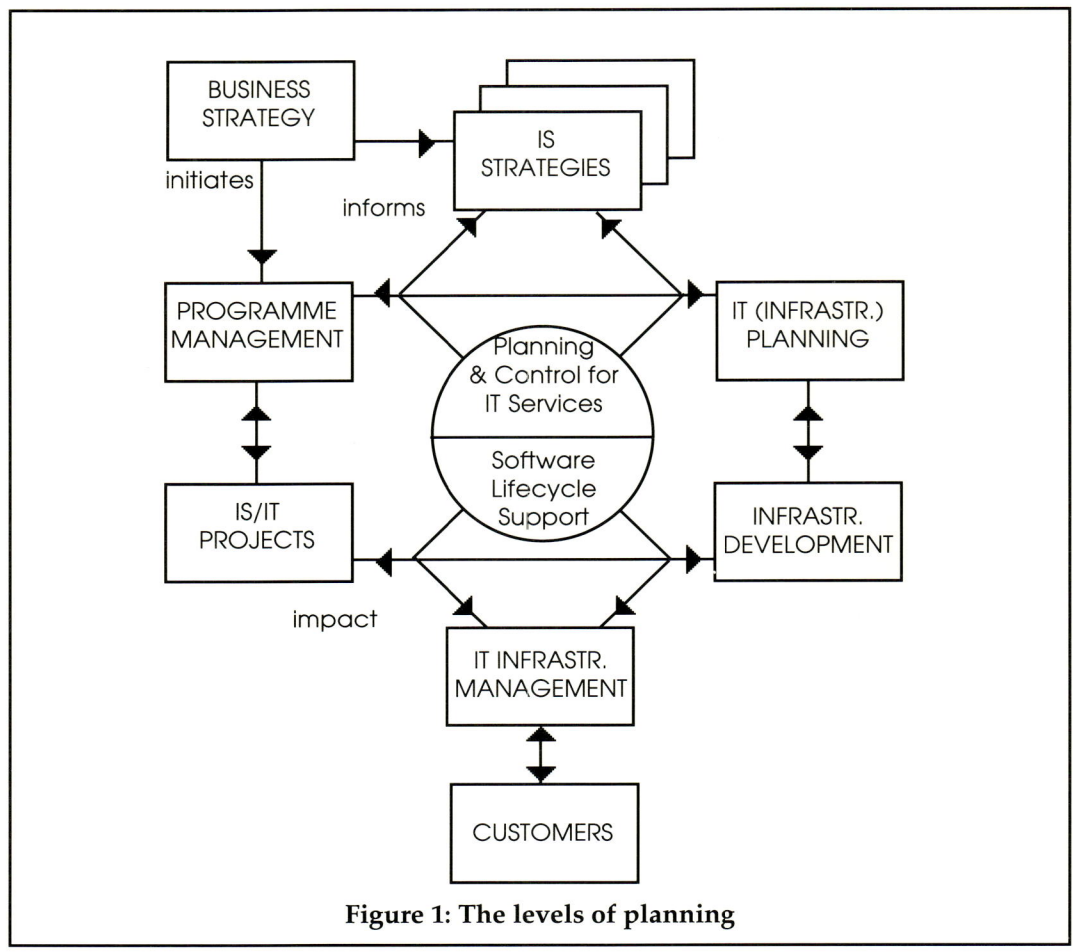

Figure 1: The levels of planning

At the next level, the demand for IT is turned into more detailed and realizable plans of action.

The programmes of work identified in the business strategy are refined into programmes of specific projects at the next level (programme planning). Changes to the supporting IT infrastructure may be managed and planned at this level (IT infrastructure planning).

Individual projects and studies are shown at the lowest level, together with IT infrastructure activities of planning and controlling the computers and networks of an organization, upon which applications systems and IT services are built and run.

Section 3
Planning for software lifecycle support

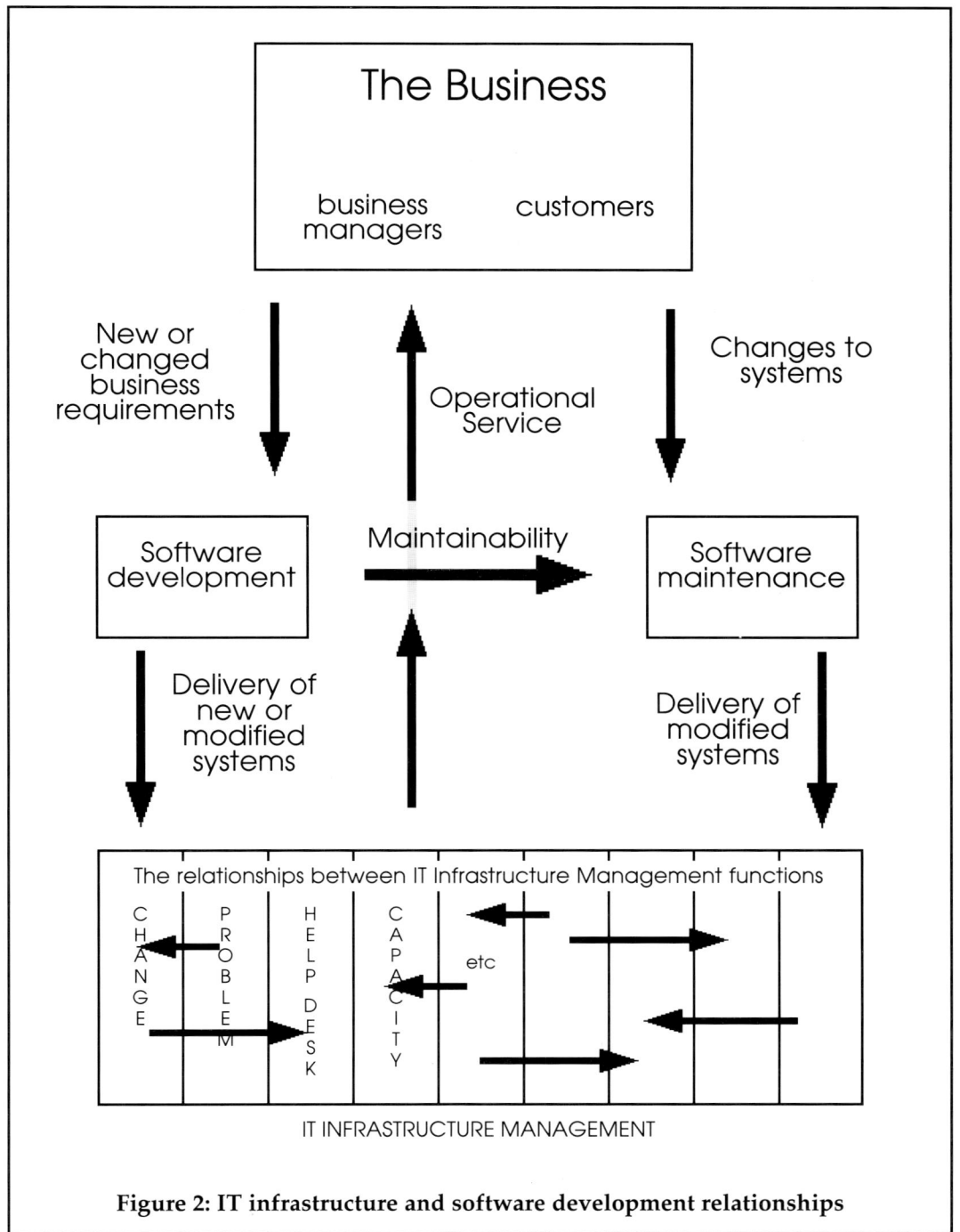

Figure 2: IT infrastructure and software development relationships

The IT Infrastructure Library
Software Lifecycle Support

The IT infrastructure management disciplines not only interact with other areas in the IT Directorate and the business, but within the IT infrastructure itself, as can be seen in Figure 2. In practice there will be many such relationships and dependencies: the most important ones are discussed in this module.

Role of the IT Planning Unit

An IT Planning Unit or a Programme Support Office would be ideally placed to coordinate the high level planning activities necessary to integrate Programme planning with software lifecycle support. Forthcoming CCTA guidance is likely to recommend that a Programme Board includes the responsibility for Design Authority, including selection and allocation of appropriate software lifecycles (in consultation with others, principal amongst whom would be software developers).

It is likely that the Programme Support Office would also monitor conformance of the planning, design and use of software lifecycles to predetermined measurement criteria. Until the guidance on Programme management is published, it is recommended that the IT Planning Unit (or Project Support Office) should be the site of the co-ordinating role. For information about the IT Planning Unit see the CCTA IS Planning Subject Guide 'The role of the IT Planning Unit'.

Monitoring of the interactions between software development and infrastructure management should be carried out by the Programme Support Office and IT Planning Unit (or the Project Support Office, if there is no IT Planning Unit). It is likely that those responsible for Infrastructure Planning and Control will also be responsible for the infrastructure management aspects of Software Lifecycle Support. It is vital that planning and monitoring activities are properly co-ordinated so that planning and lifecycle selection can be closely aligned.

There must be effective communication between:

* IS planners and IT infrastructure planners - plans for a new or revised IT infrastructure, which interface with plans for software development, may well be part of a programme of work and it is essential that the overall impact on the current IT infrastructure is assessed - see below

* IS planners and IT planners in the IT Planning Unit - so that appropriate software lifecycle models can be selected for use in the resulting IS/IT Projects

Section 3
Planning for software lifecycle support

* IT Planning Unit and software developers - to participate in selection of the appropriate software lifecycle models and to identify key milestones

* IT Planning Unit and IT infrastructure planners - to agree appropriate milestones and the interfaces between software lifecycle support models and IT infrastructure plans

* IT infrastructure managers and software developers - to identify in detail the key interfaces and how best to co-ordinate software lifecycle support activities. The Service Activity Matrix (SAM), see 3.1.6, will be of assistance.

To illustrate the relationships which might exist between development, maintenance and IT infrastructure management, a 'what could go wrong' scenario is described in Annex B.

3.0.2 Using software lifecycle models

When the introduction of a new IT system is being planned or is to be built, installed and operated, the work should be planned so that activities take place in the most appropriate order, and in a way that minimizes risk and increases quality. The resulting logical plan for the project is known as a software lifecycle model. A software lifecycle model provides the structure within which the following can be identified:

* what major activities have to be done

* what the dependencies are between them: (A must be done after B, C can be done at the same time as D, E must be repeated until some condition holds, either F or G must be done depending on some condition)

* what major products the major activities will create

* major milestones - that is, at what point products will be delivered.

A software lifecycle model is different from a project plan in one significant way. A software lifecycle model can be interpreted in many different ways because it has decision points and iterations in it, and the outcome might not be finalized until the project is under way. A project plan is a single representation and is a management tool showing which activities will take place in which order - it will not be open-ended. A software lifecycle model can be viewed as a program or algorithm which could execute in many different ways depending on the input data; a plan is simply one execution of the program for one set of inputs.

It follows that a rigorous plan cannot be drawn up before an appropriate software lifecycle model has been designed. The design of a software lifecycle model depends on the risks and quality requirements specific to the development or post-development project in hand. Since every project will have its own particular set of risks and quality requirements, every software project will need its own software lifecycle model to be designed for it. There is, therefore, no single software lifecycle model that can be used for all projects. Certain broad classes of development have similar requirements and some general software lifecycles can be used as a starting point for software lifecycle model design.

Annex C describes four of the most common software generic lifecycle models that can be used at the start of design:

* waterfall
* spiral
* evolutionary
* rapid prototyping.

In many organizations it is a combination of these generic examples that is used.

Plans

Once a software lifecycle model has been designed for a project, a plan can be drawn up. This involves looking at the decision points and iterations in the lifecycle and either planning only as far as can be reasonably predicted, or planning further by assuming the outcome of a decision or perhaps a limit on iteration. The resulting plan can then be resourced and scheduled in the traditional way for use in project control.

3.0.3 Relationship with other IT functions

Software lifecycle support not only affects many IT infrastructure management activities, but has a major effect on many other IT functions some of which are outlined below. Relationships with IT infrastructure management activities are described in more detail in Annex F.

Section 3
Planning for software lifecycle support

Quality management | Quality software is specified and designed with quality in mind; although self-evident, this maxim is intended to inform that it is not possible to fit the required quality and reliability at a later date. The cost of building in quality is more than offset by the saving (in cost and customer relations) in likely maintenance requirements that would result if quality requirements were ignored during development. Similarly, the availability of reliable software to customers of the IT Directorate is in turn a benefit to the external businesses served by those customers. A small up-front investment will pay large dividends.

Quality management activities should therefore take place throughout the software lifecycle. They must be built into the design, selection and management of IS products and services, if the latter is to deliver the required performance.

For detailed information about quality management, see CCTA's **Quality Management Library**.

Security management | Security must also be considered throughout the software lifecycle (as it should be with other IT Infrastructure management functions). This is particularly so during the software specification stage, as it is rarely feasible to apply protective measures to an installed application retrospectively.

The **CCTA Risk Analysis and Management Method** (CRAMM) provides a structured approach to the identification of the protective measures required for IT systems, including those for software. CRAMM should be used:

* during the system development process eg in conjunction with SSADM for determining the security features which need to be built into the software

* throughout the operational lifecycle of the system at regular predetermined intervals to ensure continued protection

* whenever any alteration is made to the software system including software enhancements.

More detailed information on security in the system lifecycle and further information about CRAMM can be found in **IS Guide: C4 - Security and Privacy** and the CCTA publication **Guidelines for Directing IT Security**.

The IT Infrastructure Library
Software Lifecycle Support

Cost/benefit assessment   Adoption of the concepts of software lifecycle support will provide the opportunity for organizations to identify at an early stage areas for which costs and benefits must be documented.

Cost/benefit assessment can be used throughout the software lifecycle. It is used to:

* support the initial business case for software development, and show management 'what-if' options, such as maintaining a system in-house or through outsourcing

* check the success of the development phase in a post-implementation review

* determine whether it is worthwhile to retrofit a new lifecycle to an existing system

* evaluate IT infrastructure management options, such as the costs of porting a system to a new IT infrastructure

* provide on-going cost/benefit profiles to show that

    - an application is economically viable

    - some remedial action is necessary to extend the useful economic life of a system

    - redevelopment is necessary.

The general steps in cost/benefit assessment are to:

* use the stages in the software lifecycle model as the decision points for estimation of costs, success factors and so on

* use a consistent method such as Function Point Analysis (FPA) or Constructive Cost Modelling (COCOMO) for sizing and estimating the costs of the development stages

* use the anticipated annual change traffic to estimate the maintenance costs during the expected systems life

* obtain from customer managers estimates of benefits which the proposed application will bring

* combine cost and benefit data in graphical models to show the cost/benefit profile over the anticipated system's life.

Section 3
Planning for software lifecycle support

The initial cost/benefit information is maintained over the life of the software. It is updated:

* at the end of the development phase as part of the Project Evaluation Report (PER)

* at periodic intervals during maintenance, or if software starts to show symptoms of poor performance (ie the cost is too much in relation to what is being obtained from the software).

3.0.4 Organizational issues

Implementing software lifecycle support in an IT Directorate may cause organizational change as teams move to new ways of working. The transition will need to be planned so that all staff are aware of their changed roles and responsibilities. The role of the IT Planning Unit, Programme Support Office or Project Support Office is vital if the process of co-ordinating and integrating previously separate activities is to be successful.

The guidance in this module is intended to help IT Directorates to make a smooth transition to software lifecycle support. It should enable an organization to rapidly absorb change with the maximum beneficial effect.

3.1 Procedures

This section gives guidance on planning the introduction of software lifecycle support. The main planning considerations are described under the headings of:

* appointment of an IT Services Co-ordinator

* assessment and selection of lifecycle models

* using a lifecycle model to plan for IT infrastructure management

* using a lifecycle model to plan for software maintenance

* application of software lifecycle support to new and existing software systems

* use of a Service Activity Matrix (SAM).

Identification and documentation of the interfaces between a given software lifecycle, customers of IT services and IT infrastructure managers is a fairly complex task. There are many IT infrastructure management disciplines that may be active at various stages in the lifecycle. There are a variety of lifecycle models that may be chosen, each with its own effects on the IT infrastructure.

The IT Infrastructure Library
Software Lifecycle Support

The approach adopted in this module is to describe generic planning procedures which can be tailored to the needs of individual projects. Whilst the scope of the module does not include detailed descriptions of project management methods, it is recommended that PRINCE is adopted where appropriate.

3.1.1 Appoint an IT Services Co-ordinator

While the IT Services Manager retains the customary areas of responsibility an IT Services Co-ordinator should be nominated with the overall responsibility of ensuring that the individual IT infrastructure managers are involved in all of the planning procedures described in the module.

There are various possible locations for this function within an organization. Ideally the function should be part of the Programme Support Office, IT Planning Unit or Project Support Office although some organizations may prefer to place it elsewhere within the IT Directorate.

Figure 1 illustrates an example of a planning hierarchy, which shows that the IT services co-ordination takes place at the infrastructure planning level. The IT Infrastructure Library **Planning and Control for IT Services** module should be consulted for more detailed guidance on how the planning is performed. It is likely that software lifecycle support will have ramifications at all of the levels illustrated.

The terms of reference for the Co-ordinator should include:

* liaising with development and maintenance managers to identify planning requirements

* liaising with IT service managers to ensure that they are aware of their involvement and responsibilities in specific project plans

* participation in the selection and application of software lifecycle models for IT infrastructure planning

* appreciation of the benefits of using software lifecycle models to plan for development and maintenance

* preparing plans for the IT infrastructure required to support individual IT systems

* monitoring the implementation of the plans

Section 3
Planning for software lifecycle support

* reporting progress to senior management and programme managers

* performing Project Evaluation Reports (PERs), Post Implementation Reviews (PIRs) and internal audits

* undertaking education and training of management and staff about the aims and objectives of software lifecycle support.

An initial plan for involving IT infrastructure management in software lifecycle support should be developed by the IT Services Co-ordinator, with the key aim of describing the effectiveness and benefits of co-operation between software developers and IT infrastructure managers. It is recommended that the plan centres initially on a pilot project as a small controlled experiment based upon the procedures in the module. The plan should include the following steps:

* running awareness seminars and briefing staff on the aims and objectives of co-ordination

* illustrating interactions with IS programme planning and the benefits to be accrued from using the concepts

* selection of a project or system for the pilot, noting that the pilot should be kept small, and may apply either to a new development or to an existing system

* development of the implementation plan for the pilot, using the planning procedures described here

* conducting a Project Evaluation Report of the pilot to determine how well it met the objectives.

Following the pilot project, decisions can then be made as to the more general introduction of co-ordinated software lifecycle support, and the scope of the plans can be widened to include more systems.

3.1.2 Assessment and selection of lifecycle models

The example software lifecycle, illustrated in Figure 3, covers development and use (production and maintenance) of an IT system. It shows where SSADM activities fit into a full lifecycle from initial planning to eventual decommissioning. SSADM is used for the development stages up to physical design and may also be used for maintenance (see the SSADM reference manuals for further details). Interfaces between SSADM and capacity planning are described in section 3.1.6.

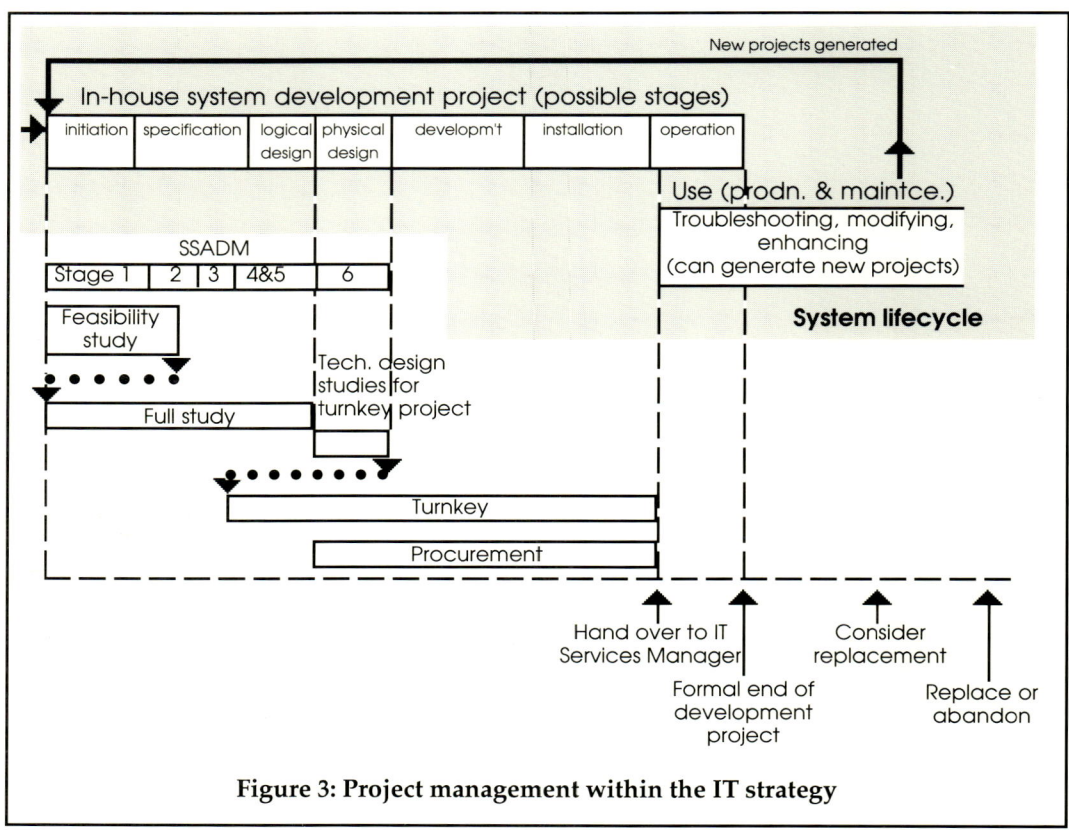

Figure 3: Project management within the IT strategy

A software lifecycle model is a management tool which provides a framework encompassing the elements of the software development and maintenance processes. It incorporates the procedures, controls and milestones from initial design through development to installation and maintenance and provides the milestones which enable progress to be assessed. Selection and use of the appropriate software lifecycle model or models is not the responsibility of the IT infrastructure managers. The Programme Support Office, in consultation with software developers, will be responsible for this task. It is essential, however, that IT infrastructure managers are aware of the selection processes and of the impact on the IT infrastructure of using a particular software lifecycle model. Annex C provides further information on software lifecycle models.

Section 3
Planning for software lifecycle support

It is strongly recommended that readers become familiar with the concepts of these models before studying the remaining procedures.

Core issues

The core issues which should be addressed include:

* what lifecycle models are available?
* how well do existing models reflect business requirements?
* is some modification of the models currently used required?
* is more than one model necessary either for an individual system, or across a range of systems?

Major considerations

It should not be assumed that a particular software lifecycle model will meet the requirements of all systems within an organization.

The following are the major considerations in the selection of a software lifecycle model:

* the model must be appropriate for the type of software system, eg whether data or function strong, transaction based or interactive, whether functional or object oriented decomposition is required
* it should be conformant with IS strategy and policy
* the model must be documented and agreed so that both quality and project management are supported
* it should define the maintenance stages clearly and in detail
* it should enable metrics to be generated for assessing key factors such as productivity and quality, see also Annex F
* it should enable cost/benefit assessment of the IT infrastructure management needed to support a software system
* the characteristics of systems which affect software lifecycle model selection should be identified, giving full weight to criteria which have the greatest importance in the maintenance stages
* there should be some consideration of assessing any existing software lifecycle models used within an organization, with the focus on the way such models affect the IT infrastructure management and the delivery of an operational service

* the treatment of modifications to a lifecycle model should be established, agreed and documented.

Annex D discusses these considerations in detail.

Whilst the developers may make the final choice of a software lifecycle model, the IT Services Co-ordinator must participate in the assessment and selection process. This will ensure that the model provides the necessary features for the planning, organization, implementation and monitoring of IT infrastructure management functions, all of which are fundamental if programme planning is to be successful.

Selection of a lifecycle model may be performed as part of a feasibility study. The criteria should include a consideration of the basic question 'Do we have the IT infrastructure to develop and maintain a system of the type proposed?'. The answer will form part of the business case for the commissioning of a new development project.

The selection of a lifecycle model may be constrained by policy decisions to standardize on specific methods. This section describes how to:

* assess the feasibility of using such models to plan for software lifecycle support

* modify a model for a particular project.

In some instances the selection of a software lifecycle model may be made retrospectively, in which case it should be carried out in conjunction with the procedure in 3.1.5 - Application to existing systems.

3.1.3 Using a software lifecycle model to plan for IT infrastructure management

This section gives advice on planning IT infrastructure management involvement once a software lifecycle model has been selected. In general, some IT infrastructure management functions are required throughout a lifecycle, some are needed only during development, and others only during operation and maintenance. Also, during a software lifecycle, the importance of a particular IT infrastructure management function may change.

Section 3
Planning for software lifecycle support

Identification and management of interfaces

There are many possible interactions between customers, developers, maintainers and the IT infrastructure management teams, and these interfaces will depend, *inter alia*, upon the particular software lifecycle model chosen and any modifications made to it. A key planning issue is identification and management of IT infrastructure management interactions. In order to do this, the following planning steps are recommended:

* identify and document where and when specific IT infrastructure management functions are active during the lifecycle

* document the tasks and deliverables required from each active IT infrastructure management functions at each lifecycle stage

* establish the size of the tasks, and estimate the resources needed and costs incurred to perform them

* determine when the tasks have to be performed, their dependencies on other tasks, and schedule them

* determine who is going to perform the tasks, and allocate resources

* identify how the IT infrastructure managers will interface within the project environment, and determine the organization required

* develop an IT infrastructure management support plan which shows the activity network, schedules, staffing, costs, timing and dependencies.

Extensions to models

Section 3.1.6 gives advice on how to document IT infrastructure management activity within a lifecycle model. The key point is that any model requires extensions to show the following interactions:

* at which lifecycle stages the different IT infrastructure management functions are active for a given project

* the detail of IT infrastructure management activity in terms of individual tasks, deliverables and resources involved.

The same level of detail is required to describe the IT infrastructure management activity as for development and maintenance. This will enable a consistent approach to be taken to project and quality management.

The IT Infrastructure Library
Software Lifecycle Support

Quality Management Systems procedures (QMS) should be planned to be implemented at appropriate stages of the lifecycle. Building in quality - as with security - is the most cost-effective means of ensuring success. Retrofitting of quality and security policies is not recommended.

Generic models

For organizations which generally use a single software lifecycle model, planning needs to be done only once to produce a generic software lifecycle dependency plan for the organization. Thereafter, it can be modified for individual projects. However, for each project, care should be taken that a model is not applied to a situation for which it was not designed.

In many cases the role of an IT infrastructure management function may change considerably as a system moves through software lifecycle stages. At the earlier stages, IT infrastructure managers are involved with setting requirements and planning for operational running of a system. During testing, the IT infrastructure managers are concerned with validating that a system will meet these requirements. During operational life, the IT infrastructure managers will be concerned with managing service levels and responding to changing requirements.

Whilst it is beyond the scope of this module to discuss individual IT infrastructure management functions in detail, Annex F describes some of the issues relating to specific ones. The purpose of the annex is to give an introduction to the major IT infrastructure management functions, and indicate how much interaction there needs to be with the developers and maintainers. Detailed information about each of the IT infrastructure management functions described in the annex can be found in other modules within the Library.

3.1.4 Using a lifecycle model to plan for software maintenance

IT infrastructure management and software maintenance are very closely inter-related. Historically, many organizations have used a lifecycle model to plan the development of systems, but not their maintenance. This has led to a number of problems:

* systems have been developed which are difficult to maintain

Section 3
Planning for software lifecycle support

* IT infrastructure managers have had to cope with additional operational problems caused by the lack of maintainability

* the maintenance process has been poorly understood and implemented, which has meant that the IT infrastructure managers have not been able to play a full role.

Two activities should be considered:

* the involvement of IT infrastructure management in the development stages of each project to ensure that maintainable systems are constructed (getting the product right in relation to maintainability)

* planning and implementing how IT infrastructure managers and the maintainers will interact during the operational life of a system (defining the maintenance process correctly).

These activities should be used concurrently with the procedures of section 3.1.3.

IT infrastructure management and software maintainability

In the context of software lifecycle support, maintainability is defined as the ease with which a software system can be corrected when errors or deficiencies are identified. The definition is extended to include modification to meet revised or new requirements.

To assess the relationship between IT infrastructure management and software maintainability, two key questions need to be answered:

* how does software maintainability affect IT infrastructure management?

* how can software maintainability be managed to include IT infrastructure management requirements?

Software maintainability, or the lack of it, may affect IT infrastructure management in many ways. Some examples are:

* unmaintainable software may become unstable, leading to an increase in incidents, and increased workloads on IT infrastructure management disciplines such as Help Desk, service level management, computer operations and problem management

The IT Infrastructure Library
Software Lifecycle Support

* with software that is difficult to change, the time taken to repair production failures may become unacceptable, leading to degraded service levels

* software with degraded maintainability may become increasingly difficult to test, leading to excessive costs and resources needed for operational testing.

Software maintainability is a quality issue. That is, maintainability requirements must be specified, implemented and validated during the development stages, under the control of a quality management system. Some requirements will be determined by maintainers, some by infrastructure management staff, and some may be common to both.

Planning for maintainability should be considered in four main stages, on a project by project basis:

* determine maintainability requirements from the IT infrastructure management viewpoint

* review the implementation of these requirements during the design and development stages

* validate the requirements during operational testing

* review the requirements with the benefit of practical experience

* continue to apply the first three stages to changes made during the production life of a system.

The same notations for documenting service activity which are described in sections 3.1.3 and 3.1.6 should be applied here. From this approach, the detailed interaction of individual IT infrastructure management functions can be identified and planned to ensure that maintainability issues are addressed throughout the software lifecycle.

In determining these interactions, additional thought should be given to the stages and activities where IT infrastructure managers should interact with maintainers.

IT infrastructure management and the maintenance process

This section is concerned with interaction between IT infrastructure management functions and the maintenance process.

In summary, the approach is to use change management procedures to document the maintenance of software. The stages of specifying, designing and implementing a change are mapped on to the change management process.

Section 3
Planning for software lifecycle support

(See the IT Infrastructure Library module **Change Management** for further information).

The stages should be described in the same way as they were for development. This not only promotes the concept of maintenance and maintainability as part of continued development, but enables the continued involvement of IT infrastructure management during maintenance.

The aim is to extend the use of lifecycle models. Too often, maintenance has been shown as a single process which follows the development stages and is not extended throughout the software lifecycle. The lack of definition and understanding has led to the problems described earlier.

Two key questions are raised:

* what are the component parts of the maintenance process?

* how should IT infrastructure managers participate in the maintenance process?

Two steps are recommended:

* define and document the maintenance stages of a software lifecycle model in detail

* document the involvement of the IT infrastructure managers in the context of the required software lifecycle.

Section 3.1.6 gives examples of how a procedure may be applied. The first example provided is based upon the change process detailed in the Change Management module. In essence the example shows how to extend the change process description to include the design and development activities needed to implement a change. Once the change process has been defined in more detail, it is then possible to identify and document the interactions between maintainers and IT infrastructure management.

The second example relates to capacity management and includes interactions between SSADM and PRINCE.

3.1.5 Application to existing systems

The task of IT infrastructure managers in applying a new software lifecycle model to an existing system may be considerable. It can be particularly difficult if the reasons for adopting a new model are to address problems such as poor service levels, low systems availability, high machine usage and excessive IT infrastructure management costs.

The IT Infrastructure Library
Software Lifecycle Support

Applying a software lifecycle model to an existing system raises a different set of issues from those encountered in development. In particular:

* the existing lifecycle and requirements of the current IT infrastructure must be understood before a new model is introduced, noting that there may be no formally adopted lifecycle model, but a series of maintenance activities which have evolved into their current state

* service levels must be maintained during the implementation

* customers must be involved in the planning and implementation of the new lifecycle model

* the contribution of IT infrastructure management may be limited to key services, or those which are currently available

* antagonism between the relative documented priorities of the lifecycles may be identified

* implementation may have to be performed incrementally.

It may be the case that a new software lifecycle model is not required, but instead the existing lifecycle stages being used need to be modified or strengthened. The guidance below can also be applied to this situation.

Applying a new software lifecycle model to an existing system requires the participation of maintainers, IT infrastructure management staff and customers.

Annex E describes these procedures in detail. In summary, four planning steps are required to implement software lifecycle support for an existing system:

* assess and document the current situation, and determine how the IT infrastructure managers can better support the existing IT systems

* where conflicts arise between the requirements of IT infrastructure management for existing lifecycles and new lifecycles, identify priorities and report to the IT Planning Unit or Programme Support Office

Section 3
Planning for software lifecycle support

* develop the software lifecycle support appropriate to the needs of the system, which includes some software lifecycle modelling for the system, and the derivation of a Service Activity Matrix as described in 3.1.6

* plan for any remedial work, such as reverse or re-engineering, that is required to improve maintainability and other aspects which will help to improve the operational IT service.

3.1.6 Documenting IT infrastructure management activity

To support the software lifecycle model and subsequent processes some form of diagram should be generated between lifecycle stages and active IT infrastructure management functions. Figure 4 provides a suggested layout for a 'Service Activity Matrix'. This is in fact the first step in the generation of a process model and the process model could be supplied to software developers for further expansion.

The matrix would initially be presented as a blank layout. Interactions between IT infrastructure management functions and various other activities would be indicated in the matrix. As a cross check on the content, software developers could perform, for example, a plotting exercise of their own for comparison.

The relationships to be plotted will vary for several reasons:

* for each software lifecycle model, the 'lifecycle stage' axis would contain different stages in different orders

* each software lifecycle model generates its own set of relationships

* within a specific software lifecycle model there may be a number of variations, each variation causing changes to the matrix

* each IT system may have some characteristics which further modify the matrix.

The main issue is that planners, and project managers, identify the relationships with IT infrastructure management, and plan to include the staff responsible at the appropriate stages within development and maintenance.

The IT Infrastructure Library
Software Lifecycle Support

LIFECYCLE STAGE >	SF	SR	PD	DD	CO	UT	IN	PV	IM	ST	OM
SERVICE FUNCTION											
Planning & Control	X	X	X	X	X	X	X	X	X	X	X
Quality Audit	X	X	X	X	X	X	X	X	X	X	X
Managing FM	X	X	X	X	X	X	X	X	X	X	X
Customer Liaison	X	X	-	-	-	-	-	X	X	X	X
Service Level Management	X	X	-	-	-	-	-	X	X	X	X
Capacity Management	X	X	X	-	-	-	-	X	X	X	X
Contingency Planning	X	-	-	-	-	-	-	X	X	X	X
Availability Management	X	-	-	-	-	-	-	-	X	X	X
Cost Management	X	X	X	X	X	X	X	X	X	X	X
Configuration Management	X	X	X	X	X	X	X	X	X	X	X
Problem Management	X	-	-	-	-	-	-	-	X	X	X
Change Management	X	X	X	X	X	X	X	X	X	X	X
Help Desk	X	-	-	-	-	-	-	-	X	X	X
S/W Control & Distribution	X	X	X	X	X	X	X	X	X	X	X
Computer Ops Mgt	X	X	X	X	X	X	X	X	X	X	X
Testing Software for opernl use	-	X	X	X	X	X	X	X	X	X	X
Security Management	X	X	X	X	X	X	X	X	X	X	X
Network Management	X	-	-	-	-	-	-	-	-	-	-

Figure 4: Example of a completed Service Activity Matrix (SAM)

NB. The figure illustrates how a SAM might appear when completed for a particular lifecycle model. The lifecycle stages to be included will depend on the model used. Likewise, the IT infrastructure management functions to be considered will depend upon the current IT infrastructure and the nature of the project.

Key to Lifecycle stages

SF - system feasibility
SR - system requirements
PD - product design
DD - detailed design
CO - code
UT - unit test
IN - integration
PV - product verification
IM - implementation
ST - system testing
OM - operations and maintenance

Figure 4 shows the points of interaction at a high level, the software lifecycle stage. It is necessary to describe this in more detail. SSADM is a method familiar to many software developers and this method is highly suitable for enhancing the description. Another method is Tom Gilb's ETVX criteria - Entry, Task, Validate, Exit. The meanings of these terms are as follows:

* Entry - those items which must be complete before this stage can begin

* Tasks - the detailed tasks to be performed in this stage

Section 3
Planning for software lifecycle support

* Validation - the quality control activities to be performed to ensure the tasks are completed correctly

* Exit - those deliverables which must be signed off so that the stage can be terminated.

By decomposing stages to this level of detail it is possible to identify the precise involvement of developers, maintainers, IT infrastructure managers and users at any point in the lifecycle. This type of notation can be extended to include specific information about dependencies, staff involved and timescales.

How this information is represented is a matter of choice. An organization should use notations with which it is familiar. They may include tables, data flow diagrams, flow charts and process diagrams.

Change management

A problem with many software lifecycle models is that they do not describe the maintenance process in any detail. In this example, the waterfall model is mapped onto the main stages described in the IT Infrastructure Library Change Management module. (See Annex C for further information about lifecycle models).

Figure 5, overleaf, shows the main change management steps performed during each maintenance phase, and how they can be mapped onto the waterfall lifecycle model.

The aim is to satisfy two key objectives:

* maintenance work is performed, as far as possible, using the same stage definitions as in development. This provides continuity throughout the lifecycle in terms of methods and tools used

* by applying the same stages and activities, the interactions between IT infrastructure managers and maintainers can be planned and implemented using the same approach as for development.

Detailed planning of IT infrastructure management interactions can proceed using the stages in Figure 5 in conjunction with the Service Activity Matrix and other techniques described earlier, and expanding items as required to cover the interactions.

This example is based upon one assumption, that the waterfall lifecycle model can be applied to maintenance. The entire waterfall is executed for each change, so a series of waterfalls make up the lifecycle.

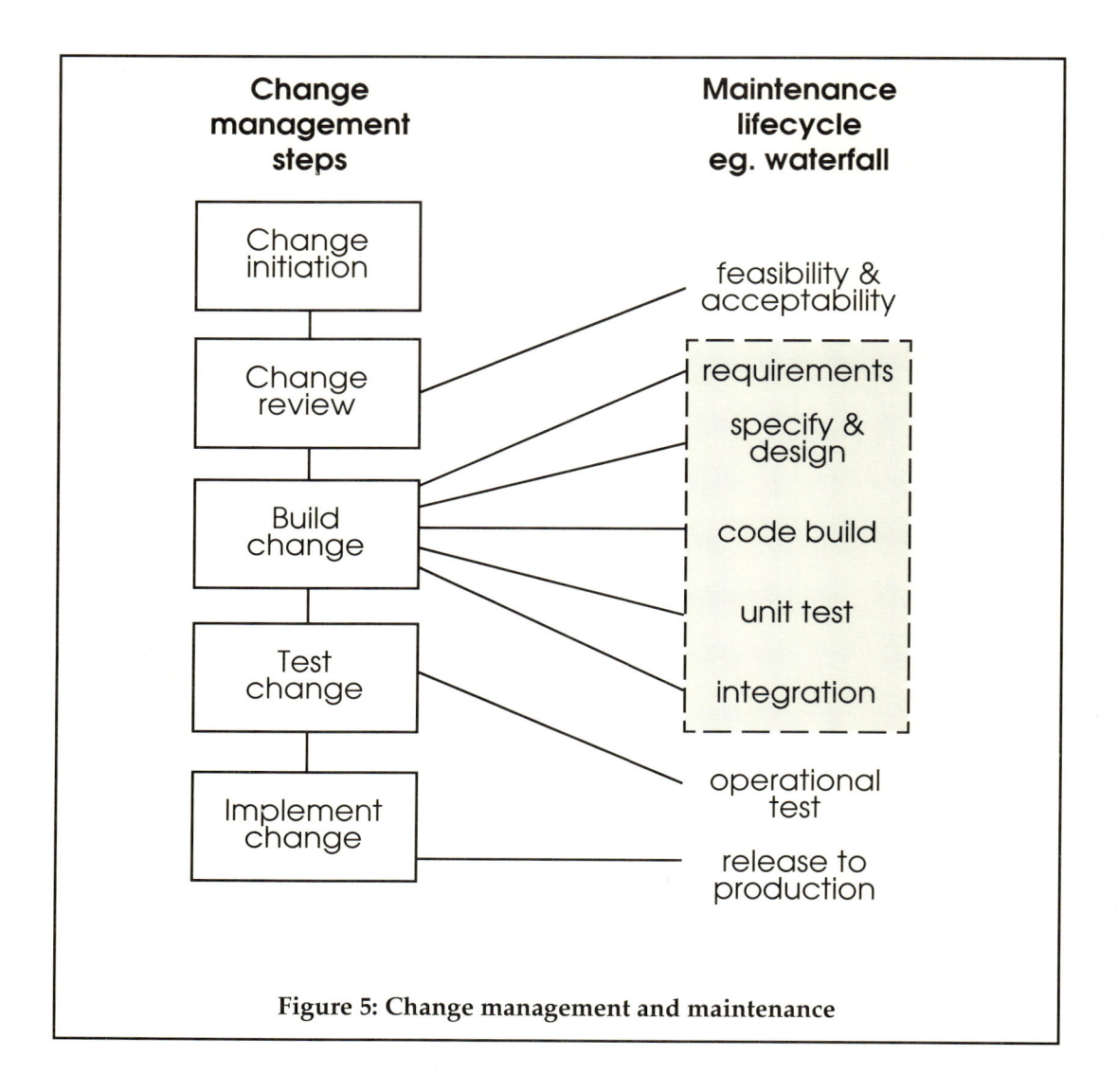

The IT Infrastructure Library
Software Lifecycle Support

Figure 5: Change management and maintenance

There may be situations when radical new requirements may be specified for an existing system, and where there is significant uncertainty about the capacity of the system to cope with them. If this is so it might be inappropriate to continue using the waterfall model, in which case the planning procedures in section 3 may be required to define an alternative model to use. This will then have to be integrated into the change management process.

Section 3
Planning for software lifecycle support

For some software systems of high complexity it may be necessary to develop a hybrid software lifecycle model, or even multiple models.

Capacity planning

This sub-section outlines the major interactions between the capacity management function and a selected software lifecycle model. The IT Infrastructure Library module **Capacity Management** and the Information Systems Engineering (ISE) library volume **SSADM and Capacity Planning** provide more detailed guidance on the subject.

Generally, the choice of software lifecycle model does not materially affect the role of the capacity manager. Software developers should be aware of the needs of the capacity manager at the earliest possible stage in the development programme. However, information systems are often designed with little emphasis on service level requirements. Cursory regard is often given for the potential size of an IT system and the impact it might have on existing information systems running alongside on the same IT infrastructure.

SSADM

SSADM concentrates on the functional definition of an information system (although some non-functional aspects are covered extensively). It has interfaces to capacity management to address the needs of capacity planning. Systems analysis provides estimates for capacity management about, for example:

* likely hardware needs - to be ratified by capacity management
* workload types
* workload volumes.

The above information is fed to capacity management at various specified stages in SSADM analysis and design. Figure 6 illustrates the major interactions between customers, capacity planners and SSADM.

The impact of new developments on the IT infrastructure can be predicted. A smooth transition from development to live running, with forecasts about likely problems enabling IT infrastructure managers to be proactive, becomes the normal way of working.

Similarly, in the maintenance process, if alterations to software are made, the capacity manager can model the effects on the IT infrastructure and make recommendations.

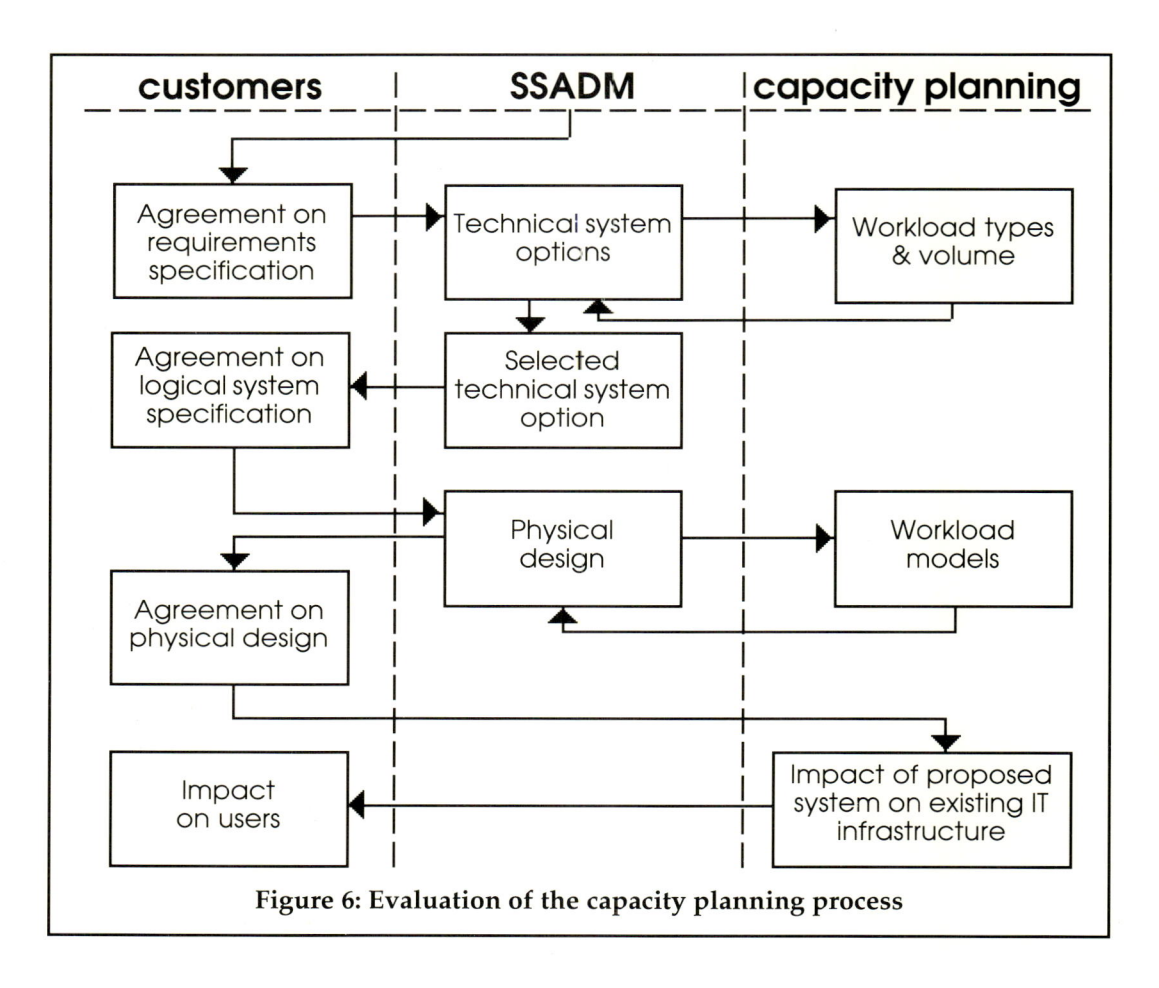

The IT Infrastructure Library
Software Lifecycle Support

Figure 6: Evaluation of the capacity planning process

| | Impact | The capacity manager will be in a position to identify the effect of changes to software on other IT infrastructure management disciplines. The capacity manager will also be aware of other projects using the techniques of software lifecycle support and will be able to assess a number of options with different input scenarios. Software models of the existing IT systems can be used to predict the effect of the changes. Conflicting developments which are likely to create problems in capacity can be identified and plans made to reduce any adverse impact. |

The ability to identify and document interactions is of major importance. The Programme Support Office or IT Planning Unit is the focal point for the co-ordination of this information to capacity management, via the IT Services Co-ordinator.

Section 3
Planning for software lifecycle support

3.2 Dependencies

This section gives guidance on identifying the dependencies to be considered when planning for software lifecycle support from the IT infrastructure management staff. There is no definitive set of dependencies since each lifecycle model generates its own, and the dependencies may be method-specific, eg SSADM drivers.

One of the key objectives of the IT Directorate is to improve the operational IT services delivered to customers. A key dependency is the commitment to the concepts of software lifecycle support from:

* the customer organization
* the IT Directorate
* IT infrastructure managers
* software developers and maintainers - this commitment should be demonstrated by the Project Board for development projects, down to project and stage managers.

The dependencies between infrastructure management functions and the software lifecycle model to be used in a given project should be planned. Figure 2 on page 13 illustrates the relationships within the IT Directorate, and between the IT Directorate and the customer's business. With some interpretation this leads to a complex set of dependencies which can be viewed in several ways:

* general dependencies, which include an understanding of the software lifecycle and how it applies to IT infrastructure management
* for software lifecycle support to start, the IT infrastructure management functions must be available - as illustrated in the Service Activity Matrix - and be ready to participate
* at different lifecycle stages there will be dependencies between the development team and the IT infrastructure management functions
* within each lifecycle stage, there will be inter-dependencies between individual IT infrastructure management functions
* within each lifecycle stage there will be dependencies between IT infrastructure management functions and the maintainers.

The IT Infrastructure Library
Software Lifecycle Support

Some of the dependencies described here are of a different nature to those discussed within other modules in the IT Infrastructure Library. The modules describing specific IT infrastructure management functions detail items that must be in place for a service to operate. This module is concerned with a wider set of dependencies which will enable IT infrastructure management to operate in unison to support development and maintenance. The IT Directorate can provide effective IT services to the customer organization if these dependencies are taken into account.

The following provides planning guidance on general dependencies, and on the more detailed service-specific dependencies.

There may be many dependencies involving:

* individual IT service managers
* developers
* maintainers
* customers.

Ancillary factors

The ancillary factors which determine dependencies are:

* the need to provide IT services to support new development projects, (ie access to development software and tools) set by the development schedules
* the priority given to any retrospective application of lifecycles to existing systems
* the requirements for mutually dependent IT infrastructure management functions such as change and configuration management either to be implemented together, or for one service to be in place before another can begin.

Whilst these factors may determine the set of dependencies, there may be organizational constraints relating to budgets and resources which modify them.

It might not be necessary to implement the entire range of responsibilities of a particular IT infrastructure management function in order for software lifecycle support to begin. For example, capacity management may be partially implemented early in the software development lifecycle, with monitoring and control milestones scheduled for implementation when a system becomes operational.

Section 3
Planning for software lifecycle support

The planning procedure in section 3.1.3 will identify many of the dependencies through the use of the Service Activity Matrix and other notations derived from the lifecycle model.

3.3 People

The planning and implementation of software lifecycle support will affect many IT staff and the customer organization. This includes IT staff in development, maintenance and the IT infrastructure management functions and also business managers and end users.

3.3.1 IT Services Co-ordinator

It is the IT Services Co-ordinator who will play the key interfacing role. This individual should be a manager within the IT Directorate, ideally with experience in:

* software development
* software maintenance
* IT infrastructure management
* lifecycle and process modelling
* quality assurance
* the use of project planning techniques.

In terms of personal skills, the IT Services Co-ordinator should have the following abilities:

* to communicate and promote the aims of co-ordinated development and software maintenance to a wide range of management and staff
* good planning and negotiating skills. A pragmatic and sensitive approach to gain the acceptance of the many staff who will be affected
* to manage without direct control, to motivate management and staff throughout the IT Directorate to fulfil their parts of the plans.

3.3.2 Staffing requirements

The planning process will need to include consideration of the impact of software lifecycle support on the work of many IT infrastructure management staff.

The staffing requirements can be assessed for each software lifecycle stage, after analyzing the requirements of the stage. A further assessment of required skills is needed at the different stages of implementation.

The required team composition can then be finalized. From this any necessary changes to the composition of IT infrastructure management teams can be identified. It will also be possible to determine where IT infrastructure management staff need to be seconded into development or maintenance teams. Finally, any new training and education needs can be assessed.

3.3.3 Organizing staff

This section does not give guidance on grades or skill levels for different roles within lifecycle stages, as there are too many geographically and organizationally dependent variables to make generalized guidance of any real value. However, the following guidance is given on potential staff organization.

The planning procedures will identify the IT infrastructure management staff required at different lifecycle stages. For these staff to work effectively with developers and maintainers, team structures are required.

The overall aim is to bring together groups of staff within an IT Directorate who need to work together. The involvement of IT infrastructure management staff should not appear to developers and maintainers as an intrusion upon their work.

It may be appropriate to organize multi-disciplinary teams, where IT infrastructure management staff are co-opted for a specific software lifecycle stage or period of time to a development or maintenance team. During this time, the IT infrastructure management staff will be required to perform the activities appropriate to each stage of the software lifecycle. They may also be required to undertake IT infrastructure management activities in support of operational IT services in parallel.

If this is not practical, specific IT infrastructure management staff could be allocated to individual development projects as a consultancy resource, which can be called upon at the appropriate times to give IT infrastructure management support.

Section 3
Planning for software lifecycle support

To increase the understanding of a co-ordinated approach to tasks undertaken by IT infrastructure management staff and developers and maintainers, consideration should be given to rotating staff through these different areas of the IT Directorate.

3.4 Timing

The IT Services Co-ordinator should be appointed as soon as a decision has been made to implement software lifecycle support.

Its introduction will be oriented around specific events. The IT workload might consist of a mix of projects about to start, development work which is at various stages of completion and systems being maintained. This section considers the most appropriate time to implement full software lifecycle support.

From a cost/benefit view, the ideal time for the introduction of software lifecycle support is at the start of a major new project, when the greatest benefits are on offer.

However, it could be over ambitious to try to implement software lifecycle support in parallel with a major software development project, which may involve implementing new software technologies and techniques. In short, such an approach may introduce too many new factors. The risk of project failure will be high and project management may become very difficult with the consequence that project schedules may be jeopardized.

Pilot projects

The recommended approach is to consider a pilot project for a new system (or phase of a system) where existing development practices are being used, and where the size of the project is not large. Although all of the major benefits discussed earlier will be unlikely to be realized using a pilot approach, the benefits are that:

* there will only be one major change, or variable, in terms of project management, which is the implementation of software lifecycle support concepts

* a project of short duration will provide quicker feedback on successes and problems

* infrastructure management resources required will be relatively small

* the risk is lower

* it is easier to manage.

Existing projects

An alternative approach is to consider a development project that is already under way. It may entail some significant re-planning of the project to enable all of the IT infrastructure management teams to participate fully. The approach may be a useful means of trialling a more limited introduction of software lifecycle support where only a small number of IT infrastructure disciplines are involved.

For application to an existing system the timing considerations must include:

* the remaining expected life of a system

* the degree of change anticipated during this life

* any problems related to maintainability.

The introduction of new IT infrastructure management disciplines (for example, the provision of an availability management function) will also affect the timing of training on software lifecycle support.

Finally, timing will also depend upon organizational constraints, such as the availability of staff resources needed to implement plans.

Section 4
Implementation

4. Implementation

4.1 Procedures

The implementation of software lifecycle support will probably be planned to be introduced over a period of time, and may involve specific projects and software development in a phased approach.

Implementation is concerned with:

* establishing the IT Services Co-ordinator and performing a pilot project

* on-going application to further projects and systems.

4.1.1 Running a pilot project

The IT Services Co-ordinator will need to play a major role in the running of the pilot project and will be required to:

* co-ordinate software development plans and IT infrastructure management plans for the duration of the pilot project

* ensure that all of the IT infrastructure management teams are involved in the pilot project at the correct times, and that IT infrastructure managers understand their individual roles

* monitor and report on progress against the software lifecycle support implementation plan

* ensure that problems are identified and resolved if possible during the pilot. Ensure that problems are not left in abeyance until the project evaluation review, although it may be necessary to do so with some problems in the pilot that could jeopardize delivery

* identify any changes that should be made to the plans and procedures during the project, and oversee these changes

* assess the progress of the pilot against the original objectives, and in particular ensure that key metrics which show the costs and benefits are recorded

* ensure that appropriate records are kept by all of the IT infrastructure managers involved so that they are available at the project evaluation review.

4.1.2 On-going procedures

The procedures required for the introduction of software lifecycle support within the organization are:

* selection of additional project and/or systems
* phased roll-out and gradual take-on of software lifecycle support for all projects
* regular monitoring and reporting on all projects
* Project Evaluation Reports (PER)
* Post-Implementation Review (PIR)
* refinement of the generic models and plans based upon experience
* continued development of cost/benefit models after the pilot to demonstrate the effectiveness of software lifecycle support, using appropriate measurements originating from the business requirements
* continued awareness campaigns and training.

4.2 Dependencies

Dependencies, like procedures, can be divided into two categories: introduction of software lifecycle support using a pilot project and those for the introduction of software lifecycle support across all of the software development projects.

The key dependency is the availability of the IT Services Co-ordinator.

The other major dependencies are:

* the preparatory procedures required to introduce software lifecycle support have been completed
* a pilot project is available
* IT infrastructure management is able and prepared to support the pilot project
* the awareness campaign has been completed
* education and training of staff has been undertaken.

Once the pilot project has been completed and software lifecycle support has been introduced, many of the issues which require resolution in order to establish software lifecycle support concepts and procedures will have been considered. The introduction of software lifecycle support

Section 4
Implementation

to other projects in the IT Directorate can be undertaken with the background and experience provided by the earlier case. The planning procedures described in Section 3 are generic, which means that once initial lifecycle models have been developed, they can be modified relatively quickly for new projects.

The dependencies affecting on-going implementation are more likely to come from organizational constraints which limit the rate of extension of the revised working practices. Examples of those constraints are:

* insufficient IT infrastructure management resources to support more than a given number of projects at any one time

* the need to phase in specific IT infrastructure management services as and when resources are available to implement them

* business pressure from the customer on the IT Directorate which limits the degree of management support available for projects.

4.3 People

Implementation requires the involvement of IT infrastructure management staff, developers and maintainers. This involvement increases as software lifecycle support is taken up more widely in the IT Directorate.

The staff requirement for a project can be determined from the planning procedures. The notations recommended for documenting the lifecycle involvement of IT infrastructure management, in terms of stages and activities (see section 3.1.6), can be used to identify which staff from individual infrastructure management functions are needed to support the different lifecycle stages.

One of the benefits of choosing a relatively small pilot project is that the number of staff involved will be limited. This will help to minimize the management problems of control and communication.

4.4 Timing

With the IT Services Co-ordinator in post, initial planning can start immediately and generic software lifecycle models can be defined. An awareness campaign can be started to inform management and staff about software lifecycle support.

The IT Infrastructure Library
Software Lifecycle Support

The timing of the introduction of software lifecycle support into a pilot project should take into account:

* the need to begin the software project as soon as possible after an awareness campaign, in order to maintain the momentum

* introduction of new IT infrastructure management functions which are needed to assist with the software lifecycle support pilot project

* availability of suitable staff and their training programmes.

As a guide, the elapsed time from the appointment of the IT Services Co-ordinator to the completion of a pilot project should be in the range of six to eighteen months. This range is suggested because the first attempts at introducing software lifecycle support concepts and procedures to IT infrastructure management and to a software development project should be considered as a short duration project.

The work undertaken to introduce software lifecycle support in the pilot project is likely to raise many issues which need to be resolved before proceeding with other projects. The longer the pilot project, the more difficult this is likely to be as the earlier stages of the pilot recede into history. However, early confirmation that the concepts and procedures are both practical and cost-effective, so that benefits can be realized as soon as possible on other projects would be helpful.

The timing of implementation for subsequent projects depends on a number of factors:

* as IT infrastructure management functions are implemented and mature, so the ability of IT infrastructure management to support more development and maintenance projects will increase

* from the pilot project, and other early projects, accumulated experience will help IT infrastructure managers to set priorities for applying the fresh approach to new and existing systems

* as the benefits become more apparent, managers will be in a stronger position to justify acceleration of the introduction of software lifecycle support

* customer requirements for new systems may dictate the timing of future implementations.

5. Post-implementation review and audit

5.1 Procedures

Project Evaluation Reports (PERs) or Post-Implementation Reviews (PIRs) covering the introduction of software lifecycle support cannot wait until the entire software lifecycle on any one project is complete, as a system may have a life of 20 years or more. The reviews discussed here do not include the internal assessment of individual IT infrastructure management functions, as they are described in the relevant IT Infrastructure Library modules.

The following general advice is for the organization to consider; the guidance is generic and can be viewed as the recommended regime for review of any IT infrastructure management discipline.

The IT Services Manager must ensure a coordinated approach is taken to monitoring and reporting on the IT Services organization.

Projects to introduce changes to the organizational structure, such as software lifecycle support, should be followed by reviews which seek to establish the success of the project itself (against timescales, costs etc) and of the changes it introduced (meeting objectives for better customer liaison for example).

There is a need for continuing review of the IT Services organization to assess effectiveness and efficiency - guidance can be found in the **IT Services Organization** module of the IT Infrastructure Library. Monitoring and modifying functions on a day-to-day basis is a requirement of line management.

While responsibility for reviews of specific functions will rest with function managers formal reviews should be coordinated.

The review plan should contain details of:

* Project Evaluation Reports
* Post-Implementation Reviews
* periodic effectiveness and efficiency review.

Project Evaluation Report
: The Project Evaluation Report (PER) provides an assessment of the project which introduced the new organization. It should identify:

* achievement against planned targets, critical success factors and objectives
* lessons to be learnt.

Post-Implementation Review
: A Post-Implementation Review (PIR) provides a formal mechanism to determine the extent to which the implementation project has met its objectives and realized the expected benefits.

Following the completion of the implementation phase (say after six or twelve months) a PIR should be instigated to assess, for example:

* whether software lifecycle support meets customers' needs
* whether good relationships within the IT Directorate have been formed as planned
* whether costs have been reduced.

Effectiveness and efficiency review
: At periodic intervals, annually or biannually, a review of IT Services should be carried out to confirm whether the organizational structure and methods continue to support the needs of the business. This review should take the form of an effectiveness and efficiency study of the IT Directorate organization which covers:

* how efficiently it uses resources
* whether the individual, and groups of, functions perform effectively
* the effectiveness of information flows between functions and groups
* the effectiveness of customer relations.

The review should also identify any trends relevant to the way individual infrastructure management functions may be carried out in the future.

Audits are completed to:

* determine the existence of procedures
* determine compliance with those procedures
* recommend improvements to existing procedures
* recommend adoption of additional procedures.

Section 5
Post-implementation and audit

Audits should be independently conducted by audit teams from outside of the IT Services organization.

Audit of specific infrastructure management functions is covered by relevant IT Infrastructure Library modules.

Where a Quality Management System (QMS) has been introduced, perhaps in line with quality management standards such as ISO 9000, quality audits must be planned. The **Quality Management for IT Services** module contains further information.

As the review of the pilot might be a different nature from that of subsequent software lifecycle support projects it is now described separately.

5.1.1 Review of the pilot project

The key question which the PER of the pilot should answer is whether the attempt to introduce software lifecycle support has been successful. Planning for full implementation can only proceed if the pilot project has proved to be successful; software lifecycle support can then be extended to include other projects and systems.

The PER should address the following questions in detail:

* were the terms of reference of the project met in full?

* did the cost of implementation fall within the budgetary estimate?

* what benefits were recorded (noting that there may be many sources of data, from objective measures kept by IT infrastructure managers about the performance of their own functions during the pilot, to subjective opinions of IT staff and customers)?

* what was the general conformance to the implementation plan, with special regard to estimating, scheduling, meeting deadlines and use of resources?

* were the dependencies pertaining to requirements for IT infrastructure management identified in the SAM?

* how easy or difficult was the management of the pilot, especially the need to co-ordinate the efforts of many different groups across the organization?

The IT Infrastructure Library
Software Lifecycle Support

* was quality management effective, both in terms of having procedures that were correct, and in terms of conformance to them?

* what problems were encountered during implementation of the pilot, and how were the problems resolved?

* what changes are recommended for the future, assuming that software lifecycle support is to continue?

The PER should include a recommendation to senior management on whether to proceed with the introduction of software lifecycle support concepts and procedures. The recommendation should be supported by a cost/benefit case derived from the pilot project.

5.1.2 On-going reviews

Whereas the PER of the pilot project is performed once, it is recommended that there are several stages where reviews of on-going software lifecycle support may be required:

* following customer complaints

* at the end of a major delivery phase - for example, at the delivery of a system for operational testing

* after a major milestone - for example, acceptance of a system for live running

* periodically during maintenance - for example, biennially.

Whilst the pilot project will have established the basic approach to planning and implementing software lifecycle support, reviews of on-going implementation are more concerned with the following issues:

* ensuring that the basic approach is tailored to meet the needs of specific projects

* determining whether the software lifecycle model definition and its interfaces with IT infrastructure management functions were correctly and completely understood for each subsequent project

* identifying how closely the actual implementation followed the plans

* identifying areas of resource contention, noting that as software lifecycle support becomes more

Section 5
Post-implementation and audit

widespread, its effects on the organization will grow, and these effects are likely to raise new management issues

* resolving specific difficulties in implementing software lifecycle support, which may require the internal review of a specific infrastructure management function

* assessing the benefits of software lifecycle support over an extended period of time

* measuring the on-going costs of the introduction of software lifecycle support in terms of resources and finance.

5.2 Dependencies

The major dependencies are that:

* individual customers, software developers and IT infrastructure managers have their recording and management reporting mechanisms in place

* key measures have been established and targets have been set, noting that measures will be required by customers, software developers, the IT Services Co-ordinator and individual IT infrastructure managers to record costs and benefits, and to provide objective management control

* changes made to the plans during implementation have been documented.

5.3 People

The IT Services Manager should be responsible for planning and performing reviews, but may select an independent person to undertake a review. Internal quality audit staff may be used to assist in this work. Attention should be given to the skills required to perform these reviews. There are various review techniques, and it is the choice of an organization which one is used. Most of them require an experienced chairman or moderator to control the review, to ensure that the right people are involved and are encouraged to contribute, and that documented pre- and post-review procedures are followed.

All project, stage and IT infrastructure managers involved in the lifecycle stages will be required to provide information to the reviewers.

The IT Infrastructure Library
Software Lifecycle Support

5.4 Timing

The first Project Evaluation Report (PER) should take place immediately after a pilot project.

Thereafter, Post-Implementation Reviews (PIR) should be performed at regular intervals defined by project milestones.

Section 6
Benefits, costs and possible problems

6. Benefits, costs and possible problems

6.1 Benefits

The benefits to be accrued from the introduction of software lifecycle support concepts and procedures are discussed in the following two sections. The first section concentrates on the major benefits which may derive from a pilot project. The second discusses the general benefits which an IT Directorate will obtain. Some of the more general benefits also apply to the pilot.

6.1.1 Benefits of a pilot project

The major benefit of a pilot project is to demonstrate to senior management in the IT Directorate that closer co-operation between IT infrastructure management and development and maintenance personnel is both possible and cost effective. This is achieved by demonstrating the practicability of introducing software lifecycle support and the resulting wider benefits for the IT Directorate.

A well chosen pilot will enable senior management to exercise the procedures in this module in a way that is controlled and such that early results are possible. This is very important if the commitment of all those involved with the principle of introducing software lifecycle support is to be sustained.

Whilst a successful pilot will record benefits relating to the specific project or system concerned, these are really secondary to establishing the practical viability of the concept.

6.1.2 Long-term benefits

In contrast to the pilot project, where the major benefit was to prove the concept with a relatively short project, of limited implementation scale, most of the benefits described below are those which will accrue over an extended period of time.

Adoption of the principles of software lifecycle support allows the IT Directorate to introduce quality procedures and address major security considerations emanating from the IS Strategy. Software lifecycle support will reinforce the ability of using structured methods to address these issues. In the long-term it is cost-benefit that is the crucial factor. Built-in quality and security, reduced maintenance bills and improved delivery of IT services each contribute to a quality service. The customer of IT Services should recognize an assurance that service levels are specified fully and achieved when a system becomes operational.

Meeting service level objectives in an efficient and timely way leads to three financial benefits:

* internal operating costs are reduced due to more efficient use of IT resources to support the information systems

* improved service levels will mean greater customer satisfaction and this in turn will provide an opportunity to develop the IT Directorate's business

* since maintainability is a design goal throughout the software lifecycle there will be a better match to requirements and IT infrastructure resources resulting in lower operational and maintenance costs.

Reduction in costs can be reflected in reduced charges to customers, to the benefit of the business.

For the IT Directorate there are also benefits in terms of culture. In tandem with other IT infrastructure management disciplines, software lifecycle support contributes to:

* making best use of costly human resources

* removing communication barriers, such as those that can exist between developers and maintainers within the IT Directorate, or between the IT Directorate and the customer

* promoting the idea that the organization is a team made up of groups acting together to meet the common goal of customer satisfaction with IT Services, which will foster greater mutual understanding

* developing a quality culture, where the aim of the IT Directorate is to meet customers' needs.

For the staff, there are other benefits, such as:

* better mutual understanding between customers, software developers, IT infrastructure management staff and the rest of the IT Directorate

* improved training and professional development

* improving job satisfaction and staff retention

* improving individual and team productivity.

Section 6
Benefits, costs and possible problems

6.2 Costs

When considering the issue of costs it is important to remember that software maintenance accounts for a significant proportion of IT expenditure in a typical IT Directorate. The benefits accruing from a co-ordinated approach to development and maintenance should result in overall cost savings, and more than compensate for costs incurred. It is important to recognize that the benefits and savings may accrue over a long period.

The main costs of establishing the role of IT Services Co-ordinator will be the employment related costs (the IT Services Co-ordinator and/or any liaison officers, and any increase to IT Planning Unit complement) plus those for project management and lifecycle modelling tools.

The implementation of software lifecycle support concepts raises a number of cost issues. They include:

* awareness campaigns and training programmes, where the costs will be a mixture of course development and staff time

* costs of implementation, which will vary with different lifecycle models, and during the course of a lifecycle

* costs to support individual projects and the effects on budgets. In very approximate terms, this could add between 10% and 15% to development costs. However, these up-front expenditures constitute an investment which serves to reduce operation and maintenance costs; the dominant factors in overall lifecycle costs

* finding ways of measuring the actual costs of a wide range of IT infrastructure management functions, so that the costs can be consolidated in a meaningful way

* determining how costs are to be treated (are they an overhead, or are they rechargeable to customer groups?)

* how costs should be included in cost/benefit models.

Because organizational structures vary so greatly, it is not possible to prescribe how best to determine and attribute costs. The IT Infrastructure Library module **Cost Management for IT Services** provides more information about detailed IT costing and should be consulted for further information.

6.3 Possible problems

There is a natural human distrust of, and resistance towards, change. Altering the relationships between IT infrastructure management, customers of IT Services, and software developers and maintainers represents significant change for many staff. The nature of the changes themselves, asking people to work together in new ways, may exacerbate such concerns. For example, if the developers perceive closer co-operation with IT infrastructure management as an intrusion or threat they may resist the changes.

The IT Directorate needs to find a suitable champion for the introduction of software lifecycle support. The selection of the IT Services Co-ordinator is key. However, this may not be easy, as an effective champion needs a number of skills and attributes including:

* authority
* a belief in what is being done
* demonstrable enthusiasm
* accepted credibility
* the ability to persuade others.

It will undermine the credibility of the implementation if the individual promoting software lifecycle support is not a true advocate of the approach.

Because software lifecycle support is a complex subject involving many people, there must be documented ownership of the changes to working practices. That is, individual managers should be able to clearly identify their responsibilities. Failure to ensure that the responsibilities are made clear and accepted could lead to a vague and ineffective collective responsibility.

Changes may be required to long standing working practices. For example, teams which traditionally worked independently now have to work in unison with other groups within the IT Directorate. Managers will need to use care and sensitivity in explaining the needs for change and the benefits to their staff, otherwise staff may see the changes as a threat.

Section 7
Tools

7. Tools

IT Infrastructure Library modules describing specific IT infrastructure management functions contain details of relevant tools. Implementing software lifecycle support implies some degree of integration of tools. This is considered under two headings:

* software tools for the IT Services Co-ordinator

* software tools for IT infrastructure managers.

Tools for the IT Services Co-ordinator

The IT Services Co-ordinator will need the following tools in order to perform their responsibilities. Software tools commonly used in IT Planning Units would be most suitable.

The most important of these is a project management tool which can be used to develop generic project plans for software lifecycle support. There may be different plan formats to support different lifecycle models. Usually, one of these plans will be selected and modified for a specific project.

PC-based project management tools are widely used and should be adequate for this task; however, they are frequently used on stand-alone machines. The IT Services Co-ordinator needs to amalgamate plans for software development projects with IT infrastructure management plans. The process of implementing software lifecycle support provides a good opportunity to consider development of a shared or networked planning environment and may offer an effective approach to integrating the plans of IT infrastructure management, development and maintenance teams.

The IT Services Co-ordinator will also require tools for modelling lifecycles, and decomposing them to show tasks, activities, dependencies, deliverables and staffing requirements. There are a variety of diagramming tools which may be considered.

As the lifecycle models and modelling process become better understood, an advanced approach may be applied, such as using an analyst workbench, and notations such as data flow diagrams. The latter approach has the advantage that underlying relationships can be defined and maintained. There are also a number of powerful tools available to software developers to facilitate process modelling.

The IT Infrastructure Library
Software Lifecycle Support

Tools for IT infrastructure management

From the modelling and planning process, it will be possible to identify where tools may improve IT infrastructure management work.

The plans will show IT infrastructure management tasks, and may be annotated to indicate the most manually intensive tasks. The current use of software tools can be mapped onto a plan, so that it is possible to identify the potential for further automation. For example, only performance management tools may be used in the organization. The plan may cater for the organization to expand tools use to include service level monitoring tools which are often linked to performance management tools and, at a later date, capacity management tools.

Section 8
Bibliography

8. Bibliography

8.1 References

IS Guide C4 - Security and Privacy (CCTA: John Wiley, 1989 - ISBN 0 471 92537 3)

Principles of Software Engineering Management, Tom Gilb, Addison-Wesley Publishing Company, 1988

Quality Management Library (CCTA: HMSO London, 1992; ISBN 0 11 330569 9)

SSADM and Capacity Planning (CCTA - Information Systems Engineering Library) (HMSO London, 1992 - ISBN 0 11 330577 X)

The Role of the IT Planning Unit (CCTA - IS Planning Subject Guide) (1991 - ISBN 0 946638 41 7).

8.2 Further reading

Boehm, B W (1981); Software Engineering Economics, Englewoods Cliffs, NJ: Prentice-Hall

Department of Trade and Industry (1991); The TickIT Guide. Contact DTI for details.

Gilb, T (1981); Techniques of Program and System Maintenance, ed. G Parikh, Winthrop Publishers

Jackson, M A and McCracken, D D (1982); Lifecycle Concept Considered Harmful, ACM Software Engineering Notes, Vol 7, No 2, April 1982, pp29-32

Jackson, M A (1983); System Development, London: Prentice-Hall

Lehman, M M (1980); Programs, lifecycles and the laws of software evolution, Proc. IEEE, 15 (3) 225-52

Lehman, M M, and Belady, L (1985); Program Evolution, Processes of Software Change, London: Academic Press

Lientz, B P and Swanson, E B (1980); Software Maintenance Management, Reading, Mass.: Addison-Wesley

Yourdon, E (1979), Managing the Structured Techniques, Englewood Cliffs, NJ: Prentice-Hall.

An overview of CRAMM (CCTA, 1990)

How to get the best out of CRAMM (CCTA, 1991)

The IT Infrastructure Library
Software Lifecycle Support

SSADM Version 4 Manuals - 4 volume set (NCC Manchester, 1990 - ISBN 1 85554 004 5)

PRINCE - 5 volume set (NCC , 1990 - ISBN 1 85554 012 6)

PRINCE in Small IT Projects (CCTA: HMSO London, 1990; ISBN 0 11 330542 7)

Annex A. Glossary of terms

Acronyms used in this module

CAD/CAM	Computer Aided Design/Computer Aided Manufacturing
COCOMO	Constructive Cost Modelling
CRAMM	CCTA Risk Analysis and Management Methodology
DTI	Department of Trade and Industry
FM	Facilities Management
FPA	Function Point Analysis
IS	Information Systems
ISE	Information Systems Engineering
ISO	International Standards Organisation
IT	Information Technology
ITT	Invitation to Tender
LAN	Local Area Network
LSDM	LBMS Systems Development Method (proprietary to LBMS)
PC	Personal Computer
PER	Project Evaluation Report
PIR	Post-Implementation Review
POPS	Protective Operating Procedures
PRINCE	PRojects IN a Controlled Environment
QIP	Quality Improvement Programmes
QMFITS	Quality Management for IT Services
QMS	Quality Management System
SAM	Service Activity Matrix
SDLC	Software Development Lifecycle (in this context)
SLA	Service Level Agreement
SLM	Service Level Management
SSADM	Structured Systems Analysis and Design Methodology
TQM	Total Quality Management

The IT Infrastructure Library
Software Lifecycle Support

Definitions used in this module

Adaptive maintenance	Adapting a system to fit an improved hardware or software environment.
Corrective maintenance	Correcting errors or bugs in software systems.
Facilities Management (FM)	The provision of the management, and operation and support of an organization's computers and/or networks by an external source at agreed service levels. The service will generally be provided for a set time at agreed cost.
Function Point Analysis	An application independent measure of program size.
IT Services Co-ordinator	The individual responsible for co-ordinating IT infrastructure management activities within the various software developments.
IT System	In the context of this module, IT system is used as an embracing term for the hardware and software that serve as the basis for provision of an IT service or services to customers.
Legacy systems	The term used to describe software systems which have been in use for many years.
Lifecycle	In the context of the module, lifecycle is an abbreviation for software lifecycle.
Maintainability	The attribute of a system which reflects how easily it can be changed.
Maintainability requirements	A statement of the degree of maintainability required for a given software system.
Maintenance environment	The complete environment needed for maintaining systems, including hardware, software, methods and tools, organization, staff and IT infrastructure.
Outsourcing	See *Facilities Management*.
Perfective maintenance	Changing a system to meet new functional requirements, or enhancing the system.
Preventive maintenance	Changing the system to improve maintainability, which includes reverse engineering.
Process model	A set of related activities, seen as a coherent process subject to measurement, involved in production of a model of a software system which can then be enhanced or altered.
Programme management	A group of projects that are managed in a co-ordinated way, to gain business benefits which may not be possible if the projects were managed independently.

Annex A
Glossary of terms

Re-engineering	The process of (optionally) re-constructing the design of a software system (see *Reverse engineering*) and enhancing and re-implementing that design either in a different environment or to produce more efficient and/or effective software.
Reverse (inverse) engineering	The process of re-constructing (part of) the design of a software system from program code (source or compiled).
Software	A generic term for those components of a computer system (eg a program) which are intangible rather than physical. A distinction is drawn between systems software (which is an essential component to the hardware and most often supplied by the hardware manufacturer) and applications software (which is specific to the role performed by the computer in a given organization).
Software development lifecycle (SDLC)	The period of time that begins with the decision to develop a software product and ends when an acceptable product is delivered.
Software engineering	The entire range of activities used to design and develop software.
Software lifecycle	The complete lifetime of a software system from initial conception to final decommissioning (contrast with SDLC). Software lifecycle includes enhancement and maintenance following delivery.
Software lifecycle model	A management device to plan the work for an IT system so that activities take place, in the right order, and in a way that minimizes risk and increases quality. A software lifecycle model captures: * the major activities to be done * the logical dependencies between them * the products resulting from the major activities.
Software maintenance	The modification of a software product after delivery, to correct faults, improve performance or other attributes, or to adapt the product to a changed environment.
Software method	A systematic way of performing part or all of the processes involved in a lifecycle model or stage (for example, the requirements stage, or design stage etc). Lifecycle stages are discussed in detail in Annex B.
Software product	A software entity (a program, or suite of programs).

The IT Infrastructure Library
Software Lifecycle Support

Software prototyping	Development of a preliminary version of a software system in order to allow certain aspects of that system to be investigated (often to elicit early feedback about functionality from potential users or to test technical feasibility).
Software system	One or more applications developed to perform a business function.
System	In the context of this module, system is used as an abbreviation for software system, unless otherwise qualified.

Annex B. A 'What could go wrong' scenario

The scenario described here is mostly fictitious, and is presented in general and simple terms. It is based upon experiences drawn from many projects (only the names have been altered to protect the innocent or guilty). It is intended that readers should identify with many of the issues and problems raised.

Background

An organization has developed a highly interactive transaction processing system using the waterfall lifecycle model. The system not only replaced an old batch system, but was also required to implement new business functions. During the early stages of development, two major problems were encountered:

* although the functionality of the old system had not been properly specified (or quantified), customers expected that a new system would significantly improve transaction handling

* the new business functions related to products that were still being designed (ie a firm set of customer requirements could not be documented during the early stages).

Design

The development team attempted design and implementation using the waterfall model. Because developers using this model could not understand the need for experimentation and risk assessment at each stage of the development lifecycle, it is only during later development stages that new customer requirements and design considerations can be fully identified. Retrospective attempts to cater for these issues invariably failed due to business pressures to make the system operational as soon as possible.

The effect of the failures to assess the true impact of the problems and to address them using experienced staff and an appropriate lifecycle would probably have been discovered to be:

* in development, during detailed design and coding

  - revised requirements and product design, leading to a significant amount of rework

  - whilst IT infrastructure management functions involvement in tasks such as capacity planning, operations requirements and service level objectives would be identified, the volatile nature

of the emerging system would force these
functions continually to re-evaluate their
requirements

- a high degree of change would place additional
pressures on change and configuration
management, lead to many versions of
documents and code during development, and
raise problems in assessing the impact of high
level changes on lower level design

* in coding and testing

- effort would be increased well beyond
expectations, giving computer operations a
problem in providing the necessary machine
resources to cope

- late changes in requirements and design; it would
not be possible to fully validate that all of the
service level requirements could be met by the
system

* in operation and maintenance

- unresolved development issues; many
deficiencies had to be addressed post-
implementation

- there would be a high level of defects in the
system

- instability of the system, giving severe problems
in maintaining service levels and system
availability

- unexpected numbers of system failures increases
pressure on computer operations as they attempt
to make additional time available for re-runs
without compromising other IT services

- large numbers of problems encountered by users
and operations, placing severe burdens on the
Help Desk (busy trying to understand the new
system), and on Problem Management
(attempting to contain the problems)

- security; most probably compromised during
operations, as an example, there could have been
a failure to appreciate the problems of securing
the networking parts of the system

Annex B
A "What could go wrong" scenario

- Customer Liaison; the system would offer customers little confidence, and the many changes would make it difficult for them to learn how to use the system effectively

- a large number of changes requiring post-implementation (including emergency) fixes, placing additional pressure on the change and configuration management services, and causing difficulties due to the need to integrate many parallel changes

- maintenance staff would find the new system difficult to change, partly because the original design would have been modified numerous times in development and would be a compromise, and partly because the volatility of the system would make impact analysis unnecessarily difficult.

In this fiction, the mismatch between the chosen lifecycle model and the nature of the system would make planning and control a formidable task. As development proceeded and the system was made live, so the reactive content of workload would increase considerably. This burden would have to be shared by all IT groups - development, maintenance and IT infrastructure management. Customers of IT Services would be the ultimate losers and, no matter how the IT groups attempt to ameliorate difficulties it would be likely that the confidence of those customers in IT Services would be irreparably damaged. In financial terms, the development budgets would overrun significantly, and estimates of operation and maintenance costs would be revised upwards by varying amounts.

The problems would have been addressed much more effectively if, at the start, it had been acknowledged that the project comprised two conflicting requirements.

Solution

The first requirement should have been identified as the need to develop an enhanced version of the previous system, where the requirements were well known. The second was to develop new business functions where some prototyping or similar experimentation was needed. One solution would have been a two-phased approach, with the first phase using the waterfall model, and the second either the spiral or prototyping model. Ensuring that experienced staff are involved at the earliest possible specification stages would of course be paramount in this (or any) major development work.

Annex C. Lifecycle model descriptions

C.1 Introduction

Lifecycle models are used to describe all of the stages through which software passes. They are used as the basis for both management and technical control.

For management purposes, they identify all of the stages and activities that need to be planned, resourced, scheduled and controlled in projects. For technical purposes, they help to identify the types of activities, and the methods, skills and technologies needed to execute them.

Many lifecycle models have been developed to meet the needs of different types of systems. A critical factor for successful systems development and maintenance is choosing the right model. This was discussed in Section 3. This annex describes the following models and their characteristics:

* waterfall

* spiral

* evolutionary

* rapid prototyping.

It is likely that experienced software developers would use a combination of lifecycle models in a given project. Customers of IT Services and IT infrastructure managers should look to software developers for advice.

Care should be taken to differentiate between lifecycle models and methods. For example, the waterfall model is often applied to commercial systems. There are several sets of methods available to implement this model, such as SSADM, LSDM and Yourdon. A set of methods may not implement all stages within a model, eg some cover the analysis and design stages, but not implementation and maintenance. However, with common sense each of the methods can be applied to a wide range of lifecycle models. Once more, experienced software developers will be expected to provide guidance.

To promote co-operation between customers of IT Services, infrastructure management and software developers and maintainers, lifecycle models are being used more extensively. They can be used to help identify all of the interactions between customers, IT infrastructure management and development and maintenance staff.

The IT Infrastructure Library
Software Lifecycle Support

There is a common deficiency in most models. They describe the design and development stages well, but leave maintenance either undefined, or as a single stage with no detailed definition. It is for this reason that the procedure in section 3.1.4 concentrates on the enhancement of models both to consider the maintainability requirements of IT infrastructure management, and to define the maintenance stage in detail.

The general approach taken here is to consider maintenance as on-going development, and wherever possible to apply the same stages, with their corresponding IT infrastructure management involvement.

C.2 The waterfall model

The waterfall lifecycle model illustrated in Figure C.1 is probably the most commonly used model, especially in commercial and government systems. Many software methods, such as SSADM, LSDM and Yourdon use it as their base and provide techniques for performing part or all the lifecycle stages.

The major strength of this model is that it describes feedback loops between successive stages. The aim is to reduce the rework required by minimizing feedback through many stages.

Early stages must be completed before later ones can commence. That is, the requirements and design stages have to be fully documented before coding and integration can proceed.

This approach is achievable for many commercial systems, but for interactive or end-user software the Waterfall model is often less suitable, as the requirements and design cannot always be documented fully before coding and testing takes place. What is often required is a model which supports prototyping as a means of developing and refining requirements (ie iterative development).

From the IT infrastructure management viewpoint, the waterfall model provides a good basis for planning IT infrastructure support during development due to its well defined, sequential stages. Unfortunately it does not describe the on-going maintenance stages at all well, and therefore requires enhancements if it is to be used for planning the IT infrastructure management involvement at this stage.

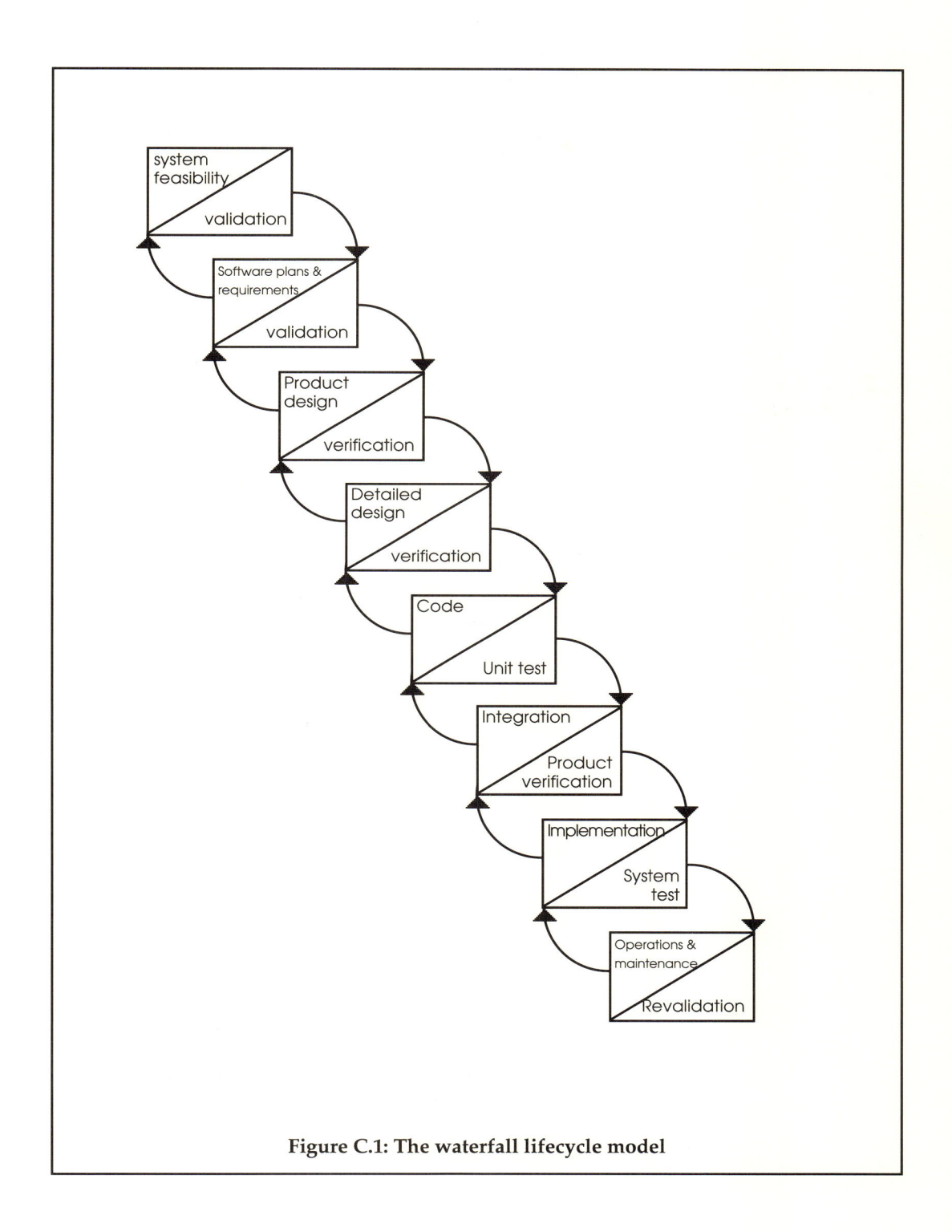

Annex C
Lifecycle model descriptions

Figure C.1: The waterfall lifecycle model

C.3 The spiral model

The usual depiction of the spiral lifecycle model is an illustration of four spiral whorls or phases, each comprising the stages of:

* determine alternatives, objectives and constraints
* evaluate alternatives and resolve risks, using prototypes
* perform a stage of development - possibly preceded by some simulations, models and benchmarks
* plan the next spiral phases.

The spiral model is a generic model, from which the waterfall model, and others, can be derived by omitting certain activities. To demonstrate this, the spiral model is described in conventional terms so that it is easier to compare with other models; the four phases of each and every spiral are described as follows:

* Initiation - what takes place when a spiral whorl or phase is started
* Risk assessment - the evaluation of alternatives and risk resolution
* Development - the actual development stages performed during that spiral whorl
* Planning - the planning of the next phase after the validation of one spiral whorl.

It is important to remember that between the planning stage at the end of one phase, and the initiation of the next phase there is a review, during which a commitment must be made to start the next phase.

A description of the main phases of this model follows, and figure C.2 shows it in graphical form.

Phase 1 - Concept of operation

Initiation	Business request for a new system - determine objectives, alternatives and constraints at this phase
Risk	Perform risk analysis, possibly prototyping some of the ideas, evaluate alternatives and resolve risks
Development	Define the concept of operation of the system
Planning	Generate a requirements plan and a lifecycle plan

Annex C
Lifecycle model descriptions

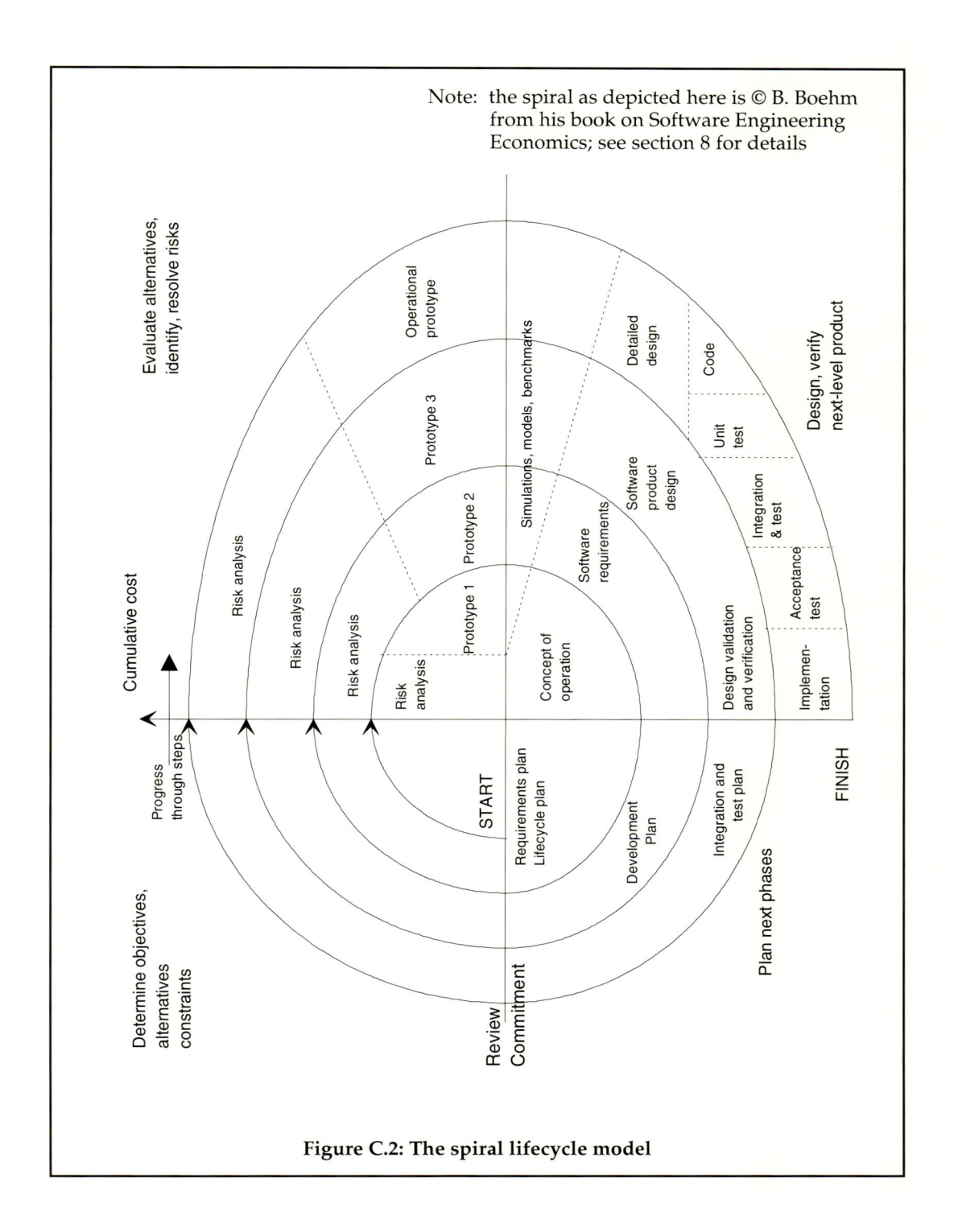

Figure C.2: The spiral lifecycle model

Note: the spiral as depicted here is © B. Boehm from his book on Software Engineering Economics; see section 8 for details

	Phase 2 - Requirements definition
Initiation	Examine the requirements plan and determine objectives, alternatives and constraints at this phase
Risk	Perform risk analysis, possibly prototyping some of the ideas, evaluate alternatives and resolve risks
Development	Software requirements analysis and definition
Planning	Generate a development plan
	Phase 3 - Product design
Initiation	Examine the development plan and determine objectives, alternatives and constraints at this phase
Risk	Perform risk analysis, producing an operational prototype to help evaluate alternatives and resolve risks
Development	Software product design, and design validation and verification
Planning	Generate integration and test plan
	Phase 4 - Detailed design, coding, testing, integration, acceptance and implementation
Initiation	Examine the design, and the integration and test plans and determine objectives, alternatives and constraints
Risk	Perform risk analysis, possibly prototyping some of the ideas, evaluate alternatives and resolve risks
Development	Detailed design, coding, unit test, integration and test, acceptance test and implementation
Planning	Plan for next phases.

Two key features of the spiral model are that in each phase there is:

* re-consideration of objectives, alternatives, and constraints before the main work of the phase starts

* risk analysis, prototyping and the use of simulations and models to help evaluate alternatives and contain risks.

The first three of the phases of the spiral model are each concerned with identifying the concept of operation, requirements and design of a system. The fourth phase contains all of the conventional development stages from detailed design through to implementation. This model places great emphasis on the early stages of development so

Annex C
Lifecycle model descriptions

that uncertainties about requirements and design can be identified and resolved before commitment to final development and implementation.

The value of the model can now be appreciated when it is applied to IT systems where the requirements are volatile. The risk analysis and prototyping activities allow an organization to understand the full implications of the IT system they are proposing. From the IT developer's point of view, it enables a set of requirements to be generated where the major issues have been identified and resolved. (Compare this with the fictitious 'What could go wrong' scenario in Annex B).

The model enables IT infrastructure managers to specify their own requirements to the development teams once risks and uncertainties have been resolved in the earlier phases. However the model, like others, lacks a definition of the maintenance stage.

C.4 Evolutionary and rapid prototyping models

Just as the waterfall model is a subset of the spiral model, so these lifecycles are variants of it too.

Organizations may select elements of the spiral model to develop their own evolutionary and prototyping lifecycle models. Also the way in which these lifecycles are executed may vary considerably from one organization to another according to the technologies available. Some methods, notably SSADM, include requirements prototyping as an inherent core and provide separate guidance on the use of other types of prototyping.

For example, in a large mainframe environment, prototyping may be performed through the use of a networked PC LAN, where analysts and programmers can develop specific functions very quickly on workstations, and then test them in the mainframe environment. IT systems developed in this way may be transferable directly into production environments. In some organizations there may be workstations which can be used to prototype new functions in a very rapid way, but where the target environment for the system may be incompatible.

The initial aims of these models should not be over-extended, eg the purpose of a prototyping environment may be to generate a functioning system which the customer can assess, and no more. If an IT system produced in this way is placed into production, then many IT infrastructure management requirements will have been ignored.

If, however, the aim is to produce a production system, then there must be clear boundaries to show at which points prototyping and IT infrastructure management become involved in the development stages (and indeed where prototyping is to be stopped). Figures C.3 and C.4 show the main stages of these models.

In terms of planning and implementing a software lifecycle, the use of these models raises a number of issues. A key question is where and how IT infrastructure managers should be involved with projects based on these models?

The purpose of prototyping may be to demonstrate functions to a customer quickly so that requirements can be refined. Consequently, a decision may be taken that IT infrastructure management concerns are not relevant at this time. Once the requirements have been agreed, thought then needs to be given as to where and how the IT infrastructure management functions are integrated with the development of a production system.

For projects using an evolutionary model, the situation is different. During one cycle of the model, the stages are explicit and lead directly to a production system. Therefore the involvement of IT infrastructure managers can be planned and implemented in a similar way to the waterfall model. However the production system is not completed in one cycle and further cycles are required. This has consequences for implementing the cooperative procedures described in this module.

The problem is that the total IT infrastructure management support required for the completed system cannot be determined until all of the evolutionary cycles have been executed.

For example, during one cycle the capacity management service may be able to successfully plan and meet the capacity needs for the production system delivered at the end of that cycle. However, as more cycles are executed, so capacity needs will accumulate to cope with the expanding system. Only when all of the cycles are complete can the total capacity requirements be assessed and by that time they may have become unacceptable.

Annex C
Lifecycle model descriptions

When the IT infrastructure management functions are being introduced during a project using the evolutionary model, additional activities may be required between cycles to assess the growing demands on the IT infrastructure, and to predict the final level of support required.

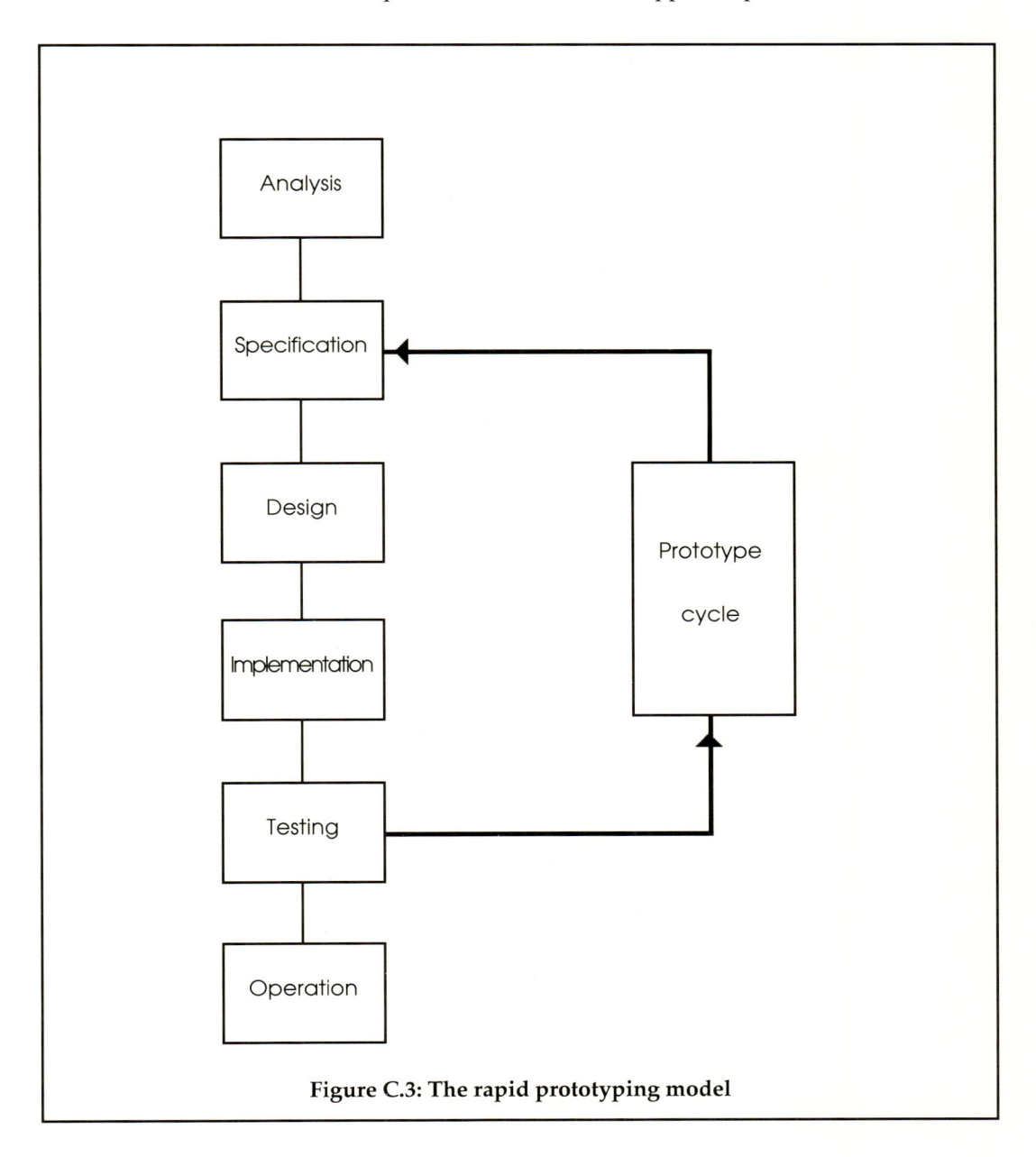

Figure C.3: The rapid prototyping model

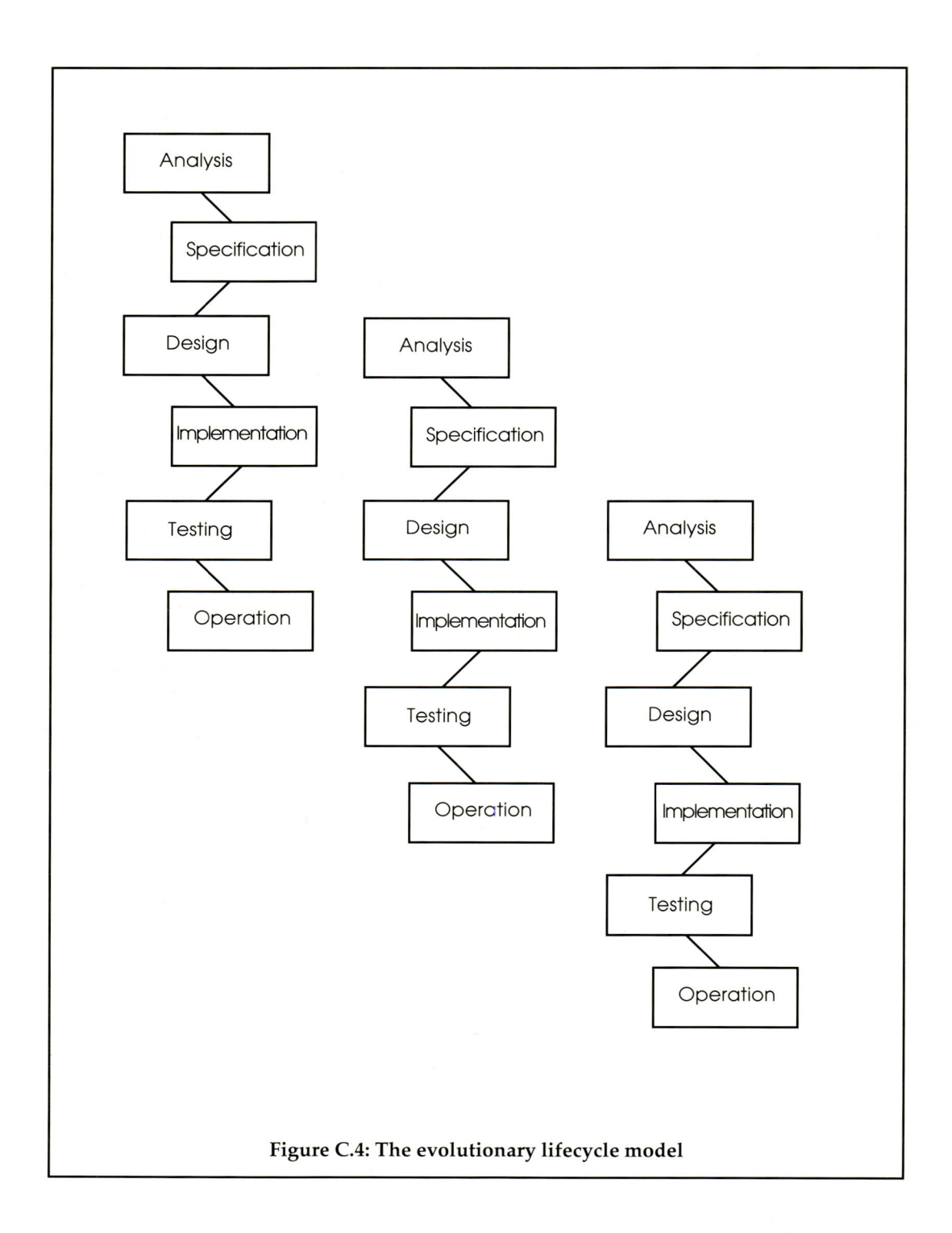

The IT Infrastructure Library
Software Lifecycle Support

Figure C.4: The evolutionary lifecycle model

Annex C
Lifecycle model descriptions

C.5 Summary

The software lifecycle model is a primary tool of the project manager, as an input to resource and timescale planning and as a means of navigation during the project. It can also be a tool for a manager procuring a development: in order to ensure quality in a system being procured, a procurer will often require that a defined, approved process is used by the developer. This is one way in which a Quality Management System certified to ISO 9001 can assist procurement. By stating a software lifecycle model at the outset, the developer can demonstrate that they have a well founded strategy for the development; during the project, the procurer can check that the developer is conforming to the stated software lifecycle model, or justifying any deviation.

It is also important to note that a method is not a lifecycle model. A method defines how activities should be carried out, and might place constraints on the software lifecycle in some way; for instance, SSADM prescribes that certain products be developed in a certain order, and to that extent constrains the lifecycle model within which it is used. Experienced practitioners of SSADM simply apply common sense when using the default process model in order to minimize the extent of any constraint.

There are underlying concerns about the use of lifecycle models if they have a prescriptive approach. Some lifecycle models, such as the spiral model, ignore the fact that systems requirements cannot be stated fully in advance, and that the development process in itself actually influences the final requirements. The model selected must therefore be appropriate and the assumptions on which it is based checked for applicability.

Annex D. Assessment and selection of lifecycle models

D.1 Introduction

This annex gives guidance on the assessment and selection of an appropriate lifecycle model for a software system. It is assumed that readers are familiar with the commonly used models (see Annex C for further details of these models).

The first task is to identify the key attributes of the proposed system. There are many which influence the decision of which lifecycle model to use. However, within many organizations, standard models, along with methods descriptions and supporting toolsets may be preferred. In this case the task of model selection is that of adapting an existing model for a new system, rather than a free choice.

The following gives guidance on how to perform assessment and selection in either of these situations. This is done under the following headings:

* system attributes
* assessment of existing models
* selection of a lifecycle model.

D.2 Systems attributes

There are several attributes which affect the decision to use a particular lifecycle model. They include:

* system type, eg batch, on-line, interactive, real-time, function strong or data strong
* the degree of uncertainty about the system's functions, ie the ability to specify the requirements
* interfaces with other systems, ie is there sharing of lifecycles?
* expected annual change traffic, eg the degree of change in response to new business needs
* timeframes for development, eg where critical schedules are involved, different models may imply different risks of meeting them
* system size, ie the general size and complexity of a system may require tailoring a model.

D.2.1 Systems type

In this context, system type means a system that is either data oriented or function oriented. The differences between these types of system in terms of lifecycle model selection are substantial.

Data oriented systems are found most commonly in commercial organizations. They reflect business processes in which there are defined sets of information upon which certain transactions are allowed to operate. A system like this could be built using SSADM. By contrast, a function oriented system is one where the base data structures may be manipulated by many types of processes. An example of this is a CAD/CAM system, where SSADM may not be the most suitable method.

Commercial or business systems are normally driven by business rules which state what data is required and how the data is to be processed. This suggests that requirements definitions and system specifications can more easily be determined with a model that uses a top-down approach.

For the highly interactive systems, such as the CAD/CAM example (and a growing number of commercial systems), there are rules governing the contents and validity of the data structures at any one time, but the user may be offered a wide range of interactive data manipulations which can be used singularly or together. As a consequence it may not be possible to produce final requirements definitions and specifications in a single pass through the stages.

D.2.2 Uncertainty of requirements

Another attribute, which is very closely related to the previous one, is whether a system can be specified with sufficient accuracy to allow a document or data driven model (eg waterfall) to be used, or whether an alternative model is required to account for greater risks of change during development.

A system may be defined as a data strong, transaction oriented system, which initially suggests that the waterfall model may be appropriate. However if the business function being considered is new and immature, eg to support a new product, then the requirements and specifications of this function may not be clear. An organization may have to consider moving away from more traditional waterfall based models to spiral based models.

Annex D
Assessment and selection of lifecycle models

D.2.3 Interfaces with other systems

The IT system, and its interfaces with other systems, may also determine the lifecycle model chosen. This is particularly so for organizations using Information Engineering techniques to generate corporate process and data models, and where there is some standardization of lifecycle models. In these cases, lifecycle models usually have to work within the constraints of the methods, techniques and tools used to execute them. Even if a sequential waterfall model is used, there is still the need in any given systems development to assess its suitability, and determine if extra stages are required to cope with unknowns and risks.

D.2.4 Annual change traffic

The expected degree of change (or annual change traffic) during operation of a system can have a significant effect upon lifecycle model selection. Where it is known that the business area supported by the system is volatile, then the chosen model must be capable of handling a high rate of change. It must lead to a relatively open design, with appropriate documentation, which allows for significant changes to be made. This consideration is probably applicable to many commercial systems, especially those with high capital investment and a long anticipated life. In this respect, the objective of the development stages is not merely to produce an operational system, but to produce one designed for change. The use of models to plan for maintenance is discussed in more detail in section 3.1.4.

D.2.5 Timeframes for development

The schedule for development and implementation of a system may also have an impact on lifecycle selection. If it is necessary to generate some systems functions in a very short period of time, then the model selected will need to enable rapid development, whilst identifying at the same time the risks being taken. A common sense approach to structured methods is another practicable solution.

D.2.6 System size

Another attribute that affects lifecycle model selection is the estimated system size and complexity. The development of large and complex systems may have to be subdivided into smaller projects, and the lifecycle model used may need to support consecutive and concurrent development. Also, larger systems may require additional activities to be specified within lifecycle stages. By comparison, it may not be sensible to break down a small project into the same level of detail as a large one.

D.3 Assessment of existing models

One way to evaluate an existing model is to analyze its effects on the management of the IT infrastructure, and the ability to deliver systems which meet infrastructure needs. Each IT infrastructure management function may contribute to this process. Some of the more prominent sources of information are:

* service level agreement reports
* system availability reports
* problem management reports
* capacity management analyses
* change traffic analysis
* productivity assessments
* cost management reports.

If a system fails to meet the requirements specified for the IT infrastructure, an internal evaluation may be made. The purpose is to assess a system's maintainability and how well lifecycle stages are implemented. A number of techniques may be used, including:

* design and code analysis measures
* documentation analysis
* methods and tools analysis
* quality audit.

From the external analysis, a view can be obtained of the effectiveness of the current lifecycle model to deliver systems which meet service requirements. From the internal analysis, reasons can be found which explain why a system does not meet them. By combining these analyses, assessments of a lifecycle model can be made in terms of its ability to:

* deliver systems which conform to specifications
* deliver systems to meet schedules

Annex D
Assessment and selection of lifecycle models

* deliver maintainable systems
* provide an acceptable maintenance environment
* manage the maintenance process.

D.4 Selection of a lifecycle model

The next stage of selection is to consider the attributes of the planned system against proposed models. This task is performed by addressing the following questions:

* are all the necessary lifecycle processes defined?
* are the processes subject to quality management?
* are the processes subject to project management?
* is the model suitable for the system type and size?
* does the model offer the required degree of productivity?
* are there acceptable methods and tools support for the model?
* does the model cover the entire system's life in an integrated way?
* does the model address risk and security issues?
* does the model allow all of the IT and business staff the right degree of involvement at different stages?
* are skills and training available for the model?

For many organizations the selection of lifecycle models will be closely coupled to corporate policies on IT development, particularly in relation to programme management standards, the specific hardware platforms being used, the methods and tools available on them, and the skills base of their staff. Some of the issues raised here may seem academic in organizations where corporate standards are firmly in place, and there is little latitude for change.

With any IT systems development project, particularly in rapidly changing business environments, it is strongly recommended that current lifecycle models are reassessed and modified where appropriate, and not simply adopted for historical reasons.

D.5 Modification of a lifecycle model

After a lifecycle model has been selected, consideration needs to be given on its detailed application to a given system or development project. This tailoring process is essential to ensure that only the relevant activities and tasks defined by a model are implemented. It is widely accepted that one of the main reasons for past failures in the use of models is a lack of thought given to their use.

What lifecycle diagrams (such as those in Annex C and many reference texts) cannot show is the number and potential complexity of the many tasks and activities which may take place within each lifecycle stage. An organization needs to have developed detailed descriptions before any tailoring can begin.

Whilst the modification process is primarily the responsibility of the development and maintenance staff, the IT Services Co-ordinator will need to ensure that the effects of any modifications are reviewed by appropriate IT infrastructure managers. This can be done using the guidance in sections 3.1.3 and 3.1.6.

Annex E. Procedures for application to existing systems

E.1 Introduction

Applying the processes of software lifecycle support to an existing system is a complex task which raises three questions:

* is there a business case to support the process?
* what degree of integration is needed and how should this be developed?
* are there maintainability issues which have an impact on management of the IT infrastructure and prompt a need for systems improvement work?

The following procedures address these questions.

E.2 Document and assess the current situation

In order to determine whether there is a business case, it is necessary to document the current situation in the following ways.

The lifecycle stages or model being used should be formalized. Particular attention should be paid to the interfaces between customers of IT Services, maintenance functions and IT infrastructure management.

All methods and tools being used to support the current model should be identified and recorded.

Project management methods used to support the model should be documented. This is often a weak area in existing maintenance and requires careful attention. The reason for this is that maintenance can be viewed as a continuous flow of work, rather than a discrete project. IT infrastructure management must manage both the operational service and the flow of changes to the systems.

The procedures described in section D.3 should be used to assess the effectiveness of the current lifecycle model and its ability to underpin software lifecycle support within the maintenance stages.

These analyses will give pointers to the interactions between the IT infrastructure managers and where the software maintenance processes require strengthening.

The IT Infrastructure Library
Software Lifecycle Support

Software maintenance managers have to measure those aspects of a system performance which may identify the need to improve software lifecycle support. They include:

* the annual change traffic on the system, expressed in terms of number and sizes of changes

* the productivity achieved with the current model and the ability of maintainers to deliver change to meet business schedules

* the inherent maintainability of the application as expressed in terms of:

    - design characteristics which help or hinder change to the system

    - the reliability and stability of the system as measured by the numbers and types of failures.

From this information, an assessment can be made of the overall effectiveness of the current model and its infrastructure support. A case can then be built for further implementation.

E.3 Enhancing strategies

If serious deficiencies are found from these analyses, then the next phase is to plan the implementation of a new or enhanced lifecycle support strategy.

To achieve this, it is recommended that the planning procedures outlined earlier are applied, but with modifications.

The major planning steps are:

* the assessment of alternative lifecycle models which can be applied to the maintenance stages

* the derivation of a Service Activity Matrix to show how the IT infrastructure management functions will interact with the new or enhanced model - see 3.1.6

* use of the generic planning procedures documented in 3.1.6 to document how each individual IT infrastructure management function will interact with the model

* identification of new methods and tools required to support the new model

Annex E
Procedures for application to existing systems

* identification and planning for the implementation issues, such as the maintaining of service levels, or the need for incremental implementation

* determining training needs for maintainers and service staff

* estimating the costs of implementation and operation of the new support strategy, and the benefits and risk associated with it.

E.4 Systems improvement work required for a new lifecycle strategy

The inability of IT infrastructure management to deliver an acceptable operational service may not just stem from inadequate lifecycle support. A major cause may be that a system is becoming inherently unmaintainable. Changes to IT infrastructure management support alone may be insufficient.

In conjunction with the planning for improved lifecycle support, it may be necessary to plan remedial work to the system itself. This work may involve the following tasks:

* analysis of documentation, followed by re-documentation of key areas

* re-engineering of programs which are both difficult to change and that are subject to most changes, where re-engineering may involve the complete re-writing of programs

* reverse engineering of the databases to identify and remove any forms of data complexity which lead to poor maintainability.

Detailed discussion of improvement projects of this nature are outside the scope of the module. From the planning perspective, it is recommended that the standard approach proposed in the module is used.

For example, if programs are to be re-engineered there is a requirement to:

* document the re-engineering lifecycle stages

The IT Infrastructure Library
Software Lifecycle Support

* determine a Service Activity Matrix showing where IT infrastructure management interacts with re-engineering lifecycle stages, bearing in mind that the lifecycle may be very similar to that of new development.

If significant re-engineering work is to be undertaken, IT infrastructure management may be concerned with issues such as:

* whether the reliability and functions of the re-engineered code can meet service level agreements
* the operational testing of re-engineered code
* the effects of re-engineered programs on capacity management.

Annex F.
Effects on specific infrastructure management functions

F.1 Introduction

This annex describes the most prominent IT infrastructure management functions in general terms, so as to provide an appreciation of how they are affected by an integrated approach.

The aim is to define briefly the purpose of each IT infrastructure management function, and to identify some of the key planning and implementation issues which need to be addressed.

For many IT infrastructure management functions it may be possible to develop generic descriptions of how a specific function interacts with a particular lifecycle model. These descriptions can then be tailored to meet the needs of an individual project. However, care should be taken to assess each project fully, so that existing descriptions are not simply assumed to be the correct ones.

For detailed descriptions of each function, reference should be made to the appropriate module within the IT Infrastructure Library.

F.2 Planning and Control for IT Services

It is assumed that planning and control mechanisms are already present within an organization. (If the mechanisms are not in place, readers are referred to the IT Infrastructure Library module **Planning and Control for IT Services** which describes in detail how this function is implemented).

The purpose of planning and control is to ensure that individual IT infrastructure management function plans can be integrated to accommodate the needs of an overall IT Service plan and that they do not conflict with one another; the plans must be comprehensive, co-ordinated and coherent.

There are strong links between planning & control and Infrastructure Planning. It also has particular relevance to:

* base level IT infrastructure plans, which describe the overall budgets, resources, accommodation and IT capacity required

* plans for individual IT services (ie services delivered to the customer), describing objectives such as availability targets, budgetary limits, service level targets.

The co-ordination task is to:

* ensure that IT infrastructure managers prepare plans for specific projects

* integrate those plans into the base level IT infrastructure plan and resolve any conflicts

* monitor the implementation and progress of the IT service plans as the lifecycle stages are actioned

* ensure that any changes to these plans are checked against the base plan

* provide management reports to both the head of IT services and to the project board.

F.3 Quality Management for IT Services (QMFITS)

The QMFITS module examines the IT Infrastructure Library functions in relation to the ISO 9001 standard, providing advice about how organizations can use the IT Infrastructure Library to help them obtain ISO 9001 certification. The QMFITS module also describes the audit of IT infrastructure management processes and products against standards and procedures. For any organization wishing to implement formal quality assurance, QMFITS is the essential function which advises management upon effectiveness of their quality systems.

In terms of planning for lifecycle support, the quality manager will need to:

* define the Quality Management System to be used to support the software lifecycle, which may be based upon ISO9001

* determine the Quality Plan for each systems project, covering all stages from feasibility study through to maintenance.

There may be significant variation in the application of quality procedures to different lifecycle models. For example, using the waterfall model to develop a new IT system will require quality procedures in all development

Annex F
Effects on specific infrastructure management functions

stages. By comparison, quality procedures might be difficult to apply in prototyping or simulation environments used in other lifecycle models. In this case, it is necessary to define clearly the point at which quality procedures are applicable to software being developed in this way. The exact application of quality procedures is documented in the project quality plan.

F.4 Managing Facilities Management

In general, the use of any third party in part or all of a system's lifecycle will have an impact on software lifecycle support. There may be many possible relationships between Facilities Management (FM) or Outsourcing and the IT infrastructure management disciplines.

Figure F.1 shows how responsibility for providing IT infrastructure management functions may be transferred to an FM provider. The diagram shows how the IT infrastructure management function is split from the in-house organization and run by the FM provider.

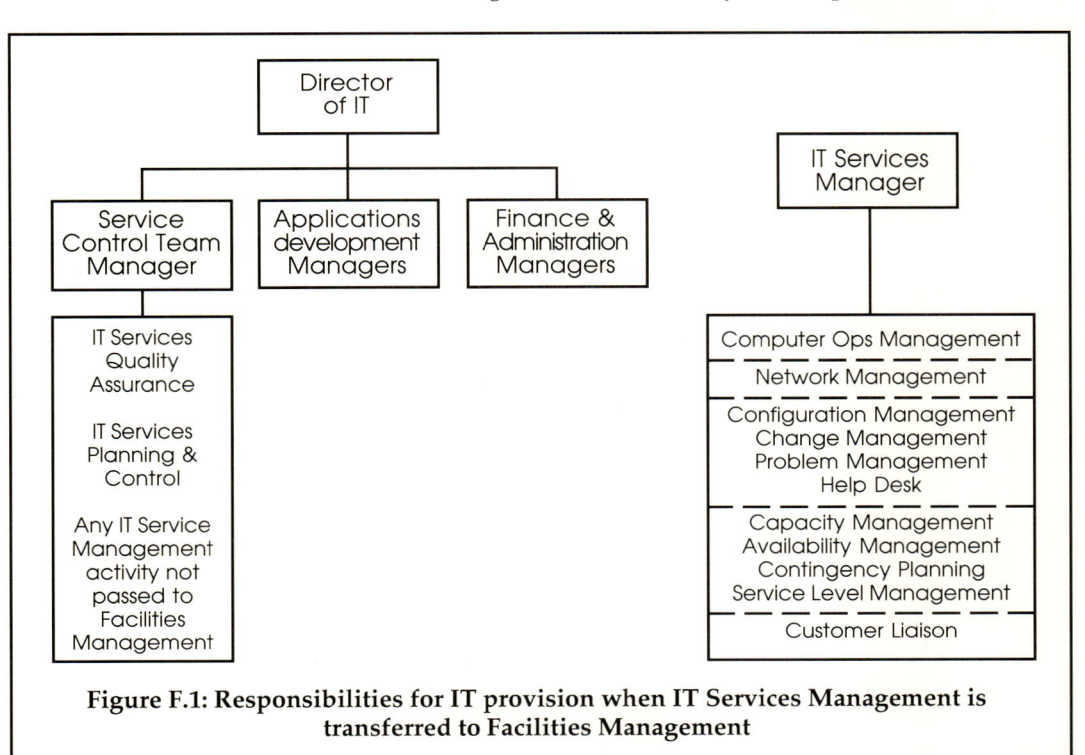

Figure F.1: Responsibilities for IT provision when IT Services Management is transferred to Facilities Management

There are several possible variations on the use of FM, which include:

* all lifecycle activities performed by the FM provider, with delivery of all IT services contracted out as well

* development performed in-house, with in-house maintenance services to support; operation and maintenance performed by a third party, with its own IT infrastructure

* development performed by a third party, but using in-house IT infrastructure resources; maintenance performed by a third party also using in-house IT infrastructure management.

Wherever a third party or FM provider is used, the in-house organization will require some form of liaison with the contractor.

For lifecycle support planning, the use of a third party does not necessarily change the Service Activity Matrix relationships for a given lifecycle model. However it will involve different people.

The selected lifecycle model and the support services identified therein, are used to control and manage any third party contracts. The model is also used in the procurement of turnkey (ready to run) systems. The requirements of implementing the model are used in the following ways:

* within an Invitation To Tender (ITT): specify methods of working, and quality and project management systems to be used

* during project work: specify the interfaces between the personnel of each company, as a basis for planning and implementing work units, and for defining deliverables

* to provide the standards for the audit of a third party. This will ensure that a third party conforms to contractual requirements.

F.5 Service Level Management (SLM)

Service Level Management (SLM) describes the function which is responsible for ensuring that the required operational service levels are provided to the customers within an organization. It is a key IT infrastructure management function.

Annex F
Effects on specific infrastructure management functions

To achieve this, service level managers must be actively involved both during development and maintenance. Service Level Agreements (SLAs) have to be specified during the development stages so that acceptance tests can be designed which validate the requirements. Service levels have, subsequently to be monitored and maintained during operation. In particular, changes to any operational system, whether software or hardware, may affect overall machine loading and have an impact on the service levels of other systems.

In general terms service level management will be involved in the following lifecycle stages:

* in feasibility studies, where initial advice may be sought about desirable service levels or a proposed system

* during requirements definition, where initial service level objectives can be defined

* during overall systems design, where architectural constraints may impact achievable service levels, and when compromises may be needed

* during system, acceptance and user testing, when it will be shown whether a system is capable of meeting SLAs

* in an on-going role during the operational life of a system (ie maintenance).

If the lifecycle model being used involves risk assessments and prototyping, then service level staff may be involved in additional tasks. For example they may be asked to assess alternative design approaches to determine which ones will best meet service level requirements.

F.6 Capacity Management

Capacity management is concerned with ensuring that computer capacity can meet the requirements of an organization. As with service level management, this function should be involved in the lifecycle at an early a stage as is possible

The key elements of capacity management are:

* performance management

* workload management

- system sizing
- resource management
- demand management.

Ensuring that there is sufficient capacity to meet service levels is an essential task. To achieve this, capacity management must be very well integrated with the development and maintenance stages.

For example:

- capacity planners will be involved in feasibility studies - assessing in general the capacity implications of proposed systems, and their effects on existing ones
- during the specification and design stages, capacity planners will be developing detailed estimates of the various hardware resources required to provide the anticipated service levels
- in acceptance testing, capacity management staff will need to verify that the actual resources required are within the bounds of the planned values (and available resources)
- during operational service and maintenance, capacity management will be concerned with ensuring that systems have appropriate levels of resource.

Capacity management may have different levels of involvement with different lifecycle models. The waterfall model supports capacity planning in the earlier development stages, on the assumption that requirements can be fixed at an early stage. With the spiral model, capacity planning may not be possible until much later in the lifecycle, when the requirements have been finally agreed and any risks resolved. See also 3.1.6.

F.7 Contingency Planning

Contingency planning describes how to plan for and recover from an IT disaster. To integrate this discipline with the system lifecycle, consideration should be given to the following:

- implementable contingency plans are needed from the start of development for the recovery of the project environment, and the continuation of development work following a disaster

Annex F
Effects on specific infrastructure management functions

* operational contingency needs have to be captured at the software requirements stage, so that their impact on design and implementation can be assessed

* during systems testing, contingency plans need to be exercised

* at handover, all operational contingency planning must be complete and verified.

Contingency plans require regular revision as new systems are developed, and during systems maintenance.

F.8 Availability Management

The availability management function is concerned with providing high levels of reliability, serviceability and availability of IT services to customers. The function is required to underpin service level agreements.

Availability management encompasses three major tasks:

* planning and managing the reliability and availability of services that will meet SLAs

* collaborating with other IT infrastructure management functions, eg problem management, proactively to improve service reliability beyond the minimum level of SLA

* overseeing contractual reliability and serviceability of supplied and maintained components and systems.

In all of these tasks, a major component, and one which is not easy to address, is that of software reliability.

Availability management functions need to be involved during both development and maintenance. During the early development stages it is necessary to define the required systems reliability. During testing for operational use, the Availability Manager will want to monitor the actual reliability of a new system against the values needed to underwrite the SLAs. Finally, during operation and maintenance, it is necessary to maintain records of reliability, growth or decay.

A key function of availability management is not only to measure current software reliability, but to identify trends. This is applicable in both development and maintenance. Consequently, the Availability Manager will work closely with the Service Level and Problem Managers.

For example, from records of errors found during development it may be possible to produce statistical predictions of improving reliability. These may be valuable indicators for determining when, and even if, a system will meet its reliability specification.

In the maintenance phase, software reliability may change in different ways. A system may stabilize and become very reliable. Alternatively reliability may decay as an increasing number of changes render the source code more fragile.

As high reliability is an inherent measure of the quality of a system, it is clear that whatever lifecycle model is used, it must support good design and coding practices. Availability management staff may have an interest in the methods and tools used by systems developers.

F.9 Cost Management for IT Services

Cost Management for IT Services describes the costing of and charging for IT services to customers. In system lifecycle terms this may be:

* the costs and charges relating to the development of systems

* the costs and charges relating to on-going operation and maintenance of systems services.

Cost management is active in all lifecycle stages. In summary the cost manager participates in:

* planning the cost management approach towards development

* providing cost management services to monitor development costs

* planning the cost management services required for operation and maintenance

* providing cost management services for operation and maintenance.

The effect of different lifecycle models upon the cost management process is likely to be small. The reason for this is that whilst costs attributable to different stages of the lifecycle may be recharged to different budgets, an organization still has to collect data, on and account for, all costs incurred during the lifecycle.

Annex F
Effects on specific infrastructure management functions

F.10 Configuration Management and Change Management

The configuration management and change management disciplines are discussed together because they are very closely linked. They describe:

* the control of all components of an IT infrastructure - configuration management

* the control of changes to these items - change management.

Effective control can only be obtained if both of these disciplines operate in unison.

The term 'component' covers all items, known as 'configuration items', which comprise an IT system. This includes source code files, objects, executables, associated documentation, test environments, system software versions, software tools versions and any other items needed to define or build the system.

From this definition, it is clear that configuration items are being written from the start of a project, eg requirements definitions, and that changes to configuration items may begin at this time. Change and configuration management functions need to be well integrated with all lifecycle stages.

The planning of these services in relation to a lifecycle model can be considered in terms of:

* controlling the configuration of a system during the development stages

* providing a definitive version of a system for formal handover to computer operations

* controlling the configuration during on-going operation and maintenance.

Ideally, the same configuration and control environment should be used for all of these stages. The main differences will be in terms of the staff and organization involved. For example:

* during the early stages of development IT infrastructure managers will be involved with defining the requirements and specifications of the IT infrastructure in relation to proposed developments

* if any of the configuration items in which they have been involved have to be reworked as the result of feedback from later stages, then it is necessary to ensure that the same staff/functions approve change requests

* at systems handover, the configuration items can be used to:

    - formally define all components of the system

    - provide audit trails for various checking purposes

    - verify that the operational system is generated from the configuration libraries

* during operation and maintenance the same control procedures should be applied.

F.11 Problem Management

Problem management is a function primarily for operational systems, although there is no reason why such a service should not be used to support systems development. It is used for:

* incident control - restoring normal service following production failures

* problem control - getting to the root cause of incidents so that they can be fully resolved

* error control - correcting problems

* management information about the above three activities.

Although problem management is active mainly during the maintenance stages, it is beneficial to define the problem management procedures required at the development stage, and to plan for its implementation.

The planning stage should determine whether an existing problem management system can be used, or if a new one is required. Care should be taken to identify all of the interactions between this function, related disciplines such as Help Desk and service level management, and the maintainers.

Annex F
Effects on specific infrastructure management functions

F.12 Help Desk

The Help Desk is a vital IT infrastructure management service which performs the following functions:

* incident control
* interfacing between customers (end-users) and the IT Directorate
* business operations support
* provision of management information.

Help Desk requirements should be specified during the development stages and implemented in time to provide an operational service.

The major planning concerns of the Help Desk stem from its tight integration with many other IT functions. Consequently, planning requires the clarification of a number of interfaces:

* operational interfaces with other functions, such as problem management and configuration management
* management reporting interfaces with other functions, such as service level management and availability management
* operational interfaces with software maintainers
* the interface with software developers to ensure that the right documentation sets are available to enable the Help Desk to function.

Another effect of the close relationship between the Help Desk and other IT infrastructure functions is that, for some lifecycle models, the Help Desk may have to be involved at several stages during the development stages. With the spiral model, service level agreements and reliability specifications may not be determined until quite late in the development. The effect of this on Help Desk planning may be to delay production of the final plan.

There is another factor which may have a significant effect on Help Desk planning, and that is the nature of the system being developed. For example, an organization may operate a centralized Help Desk service for current systems. If a new system is developed which operates through networked sites that are dispersed geographically, this service may be inadequate. There may then be a need to provide a Help Desk service on each site and a distributed Help Desk may be necessary. In this case, there will be major planning issues concerned with the implementation of such a service.

F.13 Computer Operations Management

The module **Computer Operations Management** describes the tasks of:

* the role of Operations in providing a quality service
* operability standards
* interfacing with other IT infrastructure management functions and with systems development
* application of state of the art methods for computer operations.

Computer operations management will be involved in the lifecycle in three ways:

* the provision of computer operations services to development projects
* the planning of support required for systems development
* the daily operation of live IT services.

The provision of computer operations services for development projects may be affected by a number of factors such as:

* the development environment; for example more organizations are using networked PCs to develop systems, thereby reducing the need for mainframe services
* the larger the project the greater the demand may be on computer operations, particularly if the same mainframe has to share development and production workloads
* technology changes, when computer operations may have to operate new hardware devices being used by developers.

Annex F
Effects on specific infrastructure management functions

Computer operations staff may have to participate in the following activities during the development stages:

* specifying operational requirements in terms of the procedures and job control suites needed to run a system

* specifying operational acceptance tests

* executing acceptance tests and reviewing the results

* formal handover and acceptance of a system for live running.

During the day-to-day running of systems, operations staff will require support from other IT infrastructure management functions. Some examples are:

* incident reporting should be to a Help Desk, which in turn feeds into a problem management system

* capacity and performance problems may involve the capacity management function

* the delivery of changes to software systems will involve configuration management and software control and distribution functions.

Many working relationships will be needed to help staff maintain an operational service, and these must all be identified and planned for as part of software lifecycle support.

F.14 Unattended Operating

Unattended Operating describes a range of possible modes of operation, from bridge/lights out and remote operations through to complete unattended operating.

This subject is considered to be a specialized aspect of computer operations management. It raises its own issues in terms of planning for a software lifecycle support. In particular they include:

* developing systems with the required degree of reliability to support unattended operating

* designing systems which require the minimum degree of human intervention in their operation.

The IT Infrastructure Library
Software Lifecycle Support

If unattended operating is to be a requirement, planning should include this aspect within the remit of the operations analysts involved with the overall computer operations requirements.

F.15 Testing Software for Operational Use

Testing Software for Operational Use describes the major test areas of:

* systems testing
* user testing
* installation acceptance testing.

This work is performed by an independent test authority, and assumes that programming staff have completed their own program and other integration tests.

Software lifecycle support should provide the means to bring together customers of IT services, IT infrastructure managers, and software developers and maintainers as well as software testing staff in most lifecycle stages. There should be a separate testing lifecycle (Annex C refers) which runs in parallel with the main lifecycle. For example, at the specification stage, test analysts will wish to produce test specifications based upon system specifications. As software design and implementation proceeds, so test suites may be designed and built.

An important concern will be to develop test suites which can then be used by maintenance staff.

The use of different lifecycle models will affect the involvement of operational testing functions. For example, a prototyping lifecycle places the emphasis on demonstrating system functions at an early stage of development and clearly should involve customers of IT services. Operational testing may not have a significant role to play until later in development. Any lifecycle model which is used to develop a production system must enable integration of the testing functions from the stage where systems requirements are agreed.

Annex F
Effects on specific infrastructure management functions

F.16 Software Control and Distribution

Software Control and Distribution covers:

* storage of authorized software
* release to the live environment
* distribution to remote sites
* implementation of the software.

The module promotes safeguarding of valuable software assets. The module therefore has strong links with overall management regarding security policy presented in the software lifecycle support module. The priorities as regards lifecycle modelling will be in identification of release dates and early description of security procedures for release and distribution.

F.17 Quality Management

Quality management acts as a safeguard against mistakes, reducing costs caused by wastage and the need for reworking. It focuses on the need to seek improvement in performance by enabling all personnel to collectively work for the greater good of their organization and to recognize that customer satisfaction and business objectives are inseparable.

Quality management covers quality management systems (QMS), quality improvement programmes (QIP) and total quality management (TQM), involving the following areas of activity:

* QMS implementation - planning a quality initiative, registration to ISO 9001, quality plans for guiding the quality improvement process, a quality framework and the quality infrastructure

* QMS audit - feedback and checking mechanisms for verifying the effectiveness of the QMS and reviewing progress in meeting quality objectives, collection of information to assist management reviews of the QMS and the organization as a whole

* quality training - increasing awareness of quality-related issues, providing a planned approach to the security provision of training as part of a QMS/TQM initiative and explaining the need to develop a quality culture

* quality techniques - such as problem solving, design reviews, quality circles, just-in-time and zero defects.

For detailed information about quality management, see CCTA's **Quality Management Library**.

F.18 Security

At its highest level, Security Management describes the development of an organization's security policy, and application of it to IS. In practical terms, this requires the use of a documented methodology to develop and implement a security policy.

The growing use of IT systems to support a wider range of human endeavour means that there may be many security areas to consider. They include:

* financial security, such as cheque printing or funds transfer, prevention of theft

* biological and environmental security, weapon control systems, where malfunction may threaten human life, or systems controlling chemical plants, where malfunction may lead to pollution

* commercial security, CAD systems which may contain commercially sensitive product design information

* personnel security, meeting the requirements of the Data Protection Act

* access security, prevention of 'hacking' into an application, either internally or externally through dial-in lines

* state security, the handling of information which may possess a security classification and be bound by the Official Secrets Act

* data security, within an application architecture, to ensure that programs can only access data which they need.

Annex G. Software metrics

G.1 Importance

Software metrics is the province of software maintainers and developers. Infrastructure managers may find this brief summary of the use of metrics to be of interest.

Software plays a major role in any business, from the IT systems used to provide new services to the necessary tracking and routing of information from one organization to another. Organizational success depends on the quality of software-related products and on the organization's ability to respond to its customers in a timely fashion and at a reasonable cost. Management and control of software development are essential in assuring that secure software products are built on time, within budget, and in accordance with a stringent set of quality goals.

Software metrics are essential to understanding, managing, and controlling the development process. Quantitative characterization of various aspects of development involves an understanding of software development activities and their interrelationships. In turn, the measures that result can be used to set goals for productivity and quality and to establish a baseline against which improvements are compared (perhaps identified for the PER). Measurements examined during development can point to problems that need further attention, analysis or testing. During maintenance, metrics can reflect the effects of changes in size, complexity, and maintainability. Measurement also supports planning, as projections and predictions about future projects can be made based on data collected from past projects. Tools and strategies can be evaluated, and the development process and environment can be tailored to the situation at hand.

Because metrics data collection can be laborious, software tools are essential to the process. Lifecycle models can be used to predict the times when such tools are required, and the metrics which are to be used.

G.2 When to measure

The collection of metrics should be tied to the maturity of the development process. A project can measure only what is visible and appropriate. Thus an immature project (where requirements are not well known or understood) begins by measuring effort and time, so that a baseline can be established against which improvements can be compared.

The IT Infrastructure Library
Software Lifecycle Support

Next, when requirements are defined and structured, project management metrics establish general productivity measures. Add product measurement to the project only when the process is defined well enough to support it, in this way, characteristics of intermediate products can be used to suggest the likely quality of the final product. If the project is mature enough to have a central point of control, then process measures with feedback to the controller or manager are appropriate. The feedback is used to make decisions about how to proceed at critical points in the process. Finally, the most mature projects can use process measures and feedback to change the process dynamically as development progresses.

The process maturity framework suggests metrics not only to monitor the activities in the development process, but also to help improve the process itself. By considering metrics as nested sets of measures related to process maturity, each level allows management more insight into and control over the process and its constituent products.

G.3 Metrics database

Underlying most software tools is a database, and software metrics is no exception. The software metrics database content is available to the tool and of course the database is also of historical interest.

IT Infrastructure Library
Software Lifecycle Support

Comments Sheet

CCTA hopes that you find this book both useful and interesting. We will welcome your comments and suggestions for improving it.
Please use this form or a photocopy, and continue on a further sheet if needed.

From:

              Name

         Organization

            Address

          Telephone

COVERAGE
Does the material cover your needs?
If not, then what additional material would you like included.

CLARITY
Are there any points which are unclear?
If yes, please detail where and why.

ACCURACY
Please give details of any inaccuracies found.

If more space is required for these or other comments, please continue overleaf.

IT Infrastructure Library
Software Lifecycle Support

Comments Sheet

OTHER COMMENTS

Return to: **IT Infrastructure Management Services**
CCTA,
Gildengate House
Upper Green Lane
NORWICH, NR3 1DW

Further information

Further information on the contents of this module can be obtained from:

IT Infrastructure Management Services
CCTA
Gildengate House
Upper Green Lane
NORWICH
NR3 1DW.

Telephone: 0603 694617
(GTN: 3014 4617)